LEE CANTER'S

ASSERTIVE DISCIPLINE FOR PARENTS

Revised Edition

**LEE CANTER WITH
MARLENE CANTER**

PERENNIAL LIBRARY

Harper & Row, Publishers, New York
Cambridge, Philadelphia, San Francisco, Washington
London, Mexico City, São Paulo, Singapore, Sydney

This edition was originally published in 1985 by Canter & Associates, Inc., and reissued in 1988 by Harper & Row, Publishers, Inc.

Designed by Tom Winberry

Library of Congress Cataloging-in-Publication Data

Canter, Lee.
   [Assertive discipline for parents]
   Assertive discipline for parents / Lee Canter with Marlene Canter. — Rev. ed.
      p.   cm.
   "Perennial Library."
   ISBN 0-06-096302-6 (pbk.) : $
   1. Discipline of children.   2. Parenting—United States.   3. Parent and child—United States.   I. Canter, Marlene.   II. Title.   III. Title: Assertive discipline for parents.
HQ770.4.C37 1988
649'.64—dc19   88-16243
                                                                              CIP

   89 90 91 92 RRD 10 9 8 7 6 5 4 3

To our parents, Jack and Floss, Lil and Rube, who laid the foundation for who we are today; and to our children, Joshua and Nicole, who have added such joy and meaning to our lives.

ACKNOWLEDGMENTS

A heartfelt thank you to all the staff at Canter and Associates who helped make this book possible. Special thanks to Barbara Schadlow, and, of course, Carol Provisor, my editor. We appreciate the feedback from Janie Gynn-Ornstein, Ph.D., and Nancy and Richard Levine, and, in addition, the support of Harold Roth, our agent, and Eugene Clarke at Harper & Row. Finally, we acknowledge the educators and parents throughout the nation without whose interest and support this book would not exist. Thank you all!

CONTENTS

INTRODUCTION

Assertive Discipline is the outgrowth of our combined twenty years of professional experience in helping parents and teachers to deal more effectively with the behavior of children. We brought to these efforts expertise as a teacher (Marlene Canter) and as a family-child counselor (Lee Canter).

Our initial thrust with Assertive Discipline was in the area of education. We wrote several books, including *Assertive Discipline: A Take Charge Approach for Today's Educator* and the *Assertive Discipline Resource Guide.* We developed a training workshop designed to help teachers and administrators eliminate the number one problem they face—discipline. We can gladly state that our Assertive Discipline Program has been an unqualified success. As of 1984, we and our staff have trained close to 400,000 educators (over 10 percent of all educators) from every state in the nation. The Assertive Discipline program has been endorsed or cosponsored by teacher and administrator associations in twenty-five states. Our program has received recognition from the national press, *Newsweek, U.S. News and World Report, Instructor Magazine, National Elementary Principal,* and numerous local newspapers and TV and radio stations. Most important, almost daily we receive calls and letters from grateful educators thanking us for assisting them in their efforts to help the children they teach and guide.

As the success of Assertive Discipline for educators grew, we received an ever-increasing number of requests to offer a program for parents. It was logical for us to develop this program, since our early efforts had focused on helping parents as well as educators. Our Assertive Discipline for Parents Workshops and this book are the results of our efforts. Assertive Discipline for Parents Workshops have already enabled thousands of parents to take charge at home, to the benefit of both themselves and their children. This book is the natural outgrowth of these highly successful workshops.

We want to make a few points before we get into our discussion of Assertive Discipline for Parents. For the purpose of clarity we have addressed the majority of this book to two-parent families. Throughout the book, though, you will find examples and questions related to the unique challenges encountered by single parents. Finally, we want to state clearly that the techniques and concepts presented in this book are designed to be utilized successfully by all parents.

Next, many parents equate the term *discipline* with hitting or spanking their children. We do not. We define *discipline* as a corrective action designed to help teach children more appropriate behavior. Under no circumstances should the discipline violate the physical or emotional well-being of the children.

Finally, we ourselves are parents, and our own experience has proved that the use of the philosophy and techniques presented in this book has been an invaluable aid in raising our children. But we want to add that Assertive Discipline is not a foolproof method that will enable us—or you—to be successful in all our interactions with our children. Parenting, in our opinion, is the greatest challenge an individual can attempt. We are all human, and no human is perfect. Thus, in raising our children we do the best we can despite the imperfections innate in all of us. Though Assertive Discipline is not a panacea for dealing with your children's behavior, it will prove a tremendous aid that can significantly lessen your struggle to be a good parent.

LEE CANTER'S
ASSERTIVE DISCIPLINE
FOR PARENTS

Chapter 1   **TAKE CHARGE AND BE THE BOSS**

There are times I really feel like I can't handle my kids. The way my kids carry on is simply too much for me. I talk and they just don't listen. I'm lost, I'm overwhelmed, and I'm scared.

     —Mother of two, ages seven and ten

I've tried everything I can think of to get my children to behave. I talk to them, I listen to them, I help them express their feelings, I reason with them, and they still act up and talk back day-in and day-out. I'm just at my wits' end.

     —Father of three, ages four, eight, and eleven

My kids are just too strong-willed for me or their teacher to handle. It seems that every day I get a call from school about how bad one of them has been. The teachers ask me to do something with my kids and all I can honestly say is that I don't know what to do. I can't describe how frustrating this is for me.

     —Mother of two, ages twelve and fourteen

Every day we hear comments like these from parents we work with. Why is this so? More and more parents are expressing how overwhelmed and powerless they feel in dealing with the misbehavior of their children. At times it seems that we are encountering a generation of children who are so strong-willed that in many ways they are controlling the parents who are supposed to be leading and guiding them. The result we observe in all too many families is unnecessary stress, tension and conflict.

At the same time that so many parents feel frustrated and helpless, other parents demonstrate that they are fully capable of getting their children to behave. You may ask, ''Why do those parents get their children to do what they want them to?'' We asked the same question ourselves, and after years of carefully examining parent/child interactions, we found what we believe is the answer. Parents who are effective with their children possess the skills and confidence necessary to clearly and firmly communicate their wants and needs to their children. These parents are prepared to stand up to their children's misbehavior in a firm, no-nonsense and caring manner. Basically, these parents assert their authority with their children.

In Assertive Discipline we have taken the skills we have learned from these effective parents and combined them into a systematic program designed to enable parents to take charge of their children's misbehavior in a firm, consistent and loving manner.

WHEN DO YOU NEED ASSERTIVE DISCIPLINE?

Assertive Discipline should be used when your everyday approaches to handling your children's behavior haven't worked. If talking with your children, reasoning with them or understanding their feelings doesn't help improve their behavior, then it's time for Assertive Discipline. For example:

You have visitors one evening and your four-year-old daughter is still awake at 9:30 P.M. She is overtired and irritable, but refuses to go to sleep. You understand that she doesn't want to miss the fun, but you feel it is in her best interest and your best interest that she goes to sleep. How do you get her into bed?

Your two children are continually at odds with one another. They argue, tease each other, and sometimes fight. You've tried separating them, having family meetings, understanding the reasons they feel the way they do, but the conflicts continue. You are reaching the point at which you can't take it any more. What can you do?

You have a full-time job and you need your teenage son's help with the housework. He refuses to help, saying he hates doing chores. You realize that his friends don't have these responsibilities and that he would rather play ball the entire afternoon, but you are too tired at the end of the day to do all the housework yourself. You've spoken to him at length about the issue, but he still will not do as you ask. How do you get him to help?

At times like these you need specific skills to ensure that your children listen to you. At times like these you need Assertive Discipline.

BE THE BOSS

Through Assertive Discipline we will teach you how to take charge in problem situations and let your children know you must be the ''boss.'' By being the boss we mean sending your children the following message:

I care too much about you to let you misbehave. Your problem behavior must stop. I'm prepared to back up my words with appropriate actions to let you know I mean business.

In addition, and just as important, being the boss means you care enough to provide your children with direct and positive feedback when they do change their problem behavior.

ROADBLOCKS

If in the past you have ever found it difficult to be the boss when your children's behavior demands it, don't fret—you are not alone. Many, if not most, of today's parents are in the same position. We have found that there are two major roadblocks to assertive parent behavior.

Reluctance to Come on Strong: When a parent responds in a take-charge manner, he or she typically responds to the child with a firm, direct statement. We are well aware that many parents feel they are failures if they have to respond forcefully in order to get their children to do what they want. Many parents have been told by contemporary child-rearing experts that for the well-being of their children, no matter how badly they behave, the parents should avoid "stern" or "authoritarian" actions and find alternative psychological approaches. These include talking to their children about why they misbehave (counseling approach), negotiating with their children to change the problem behavior (democratic approach), and/or praising their children only when they behave (behavior modification approach). Each of these approaches has merit; however, none of them provides you with an answer for what to do when you use them and your child still will not behave. What we are saying in Assertive Discipline is that, for those times when all else fails, it is appropriate and necessary that you put aside all your other approaches and recognize that your children need you to assertively take charge when they engage in disruptive and destructive behavior.

Not Knowing How to Take Charge: The second reason that prevents some parents from not taking charge with their children is that they just do not know how to do so. If you are like most parents, you have probably had no training in how to be a parent. You may be trying to deal with children who behave toward you very differently from the way you behaved toward your parents. We continually hear parents say, "My children act in a manner I would never have thought of doing." One father told us, "My children say things I would never even think of."

The net result of this change is that you may be unable to handle your children's misbehavior. Your learned approaches to discipline may not work, and all the new approaches you have read or heard about also may prove ineffective. In other words, you lack the needed skills and confidence to take charge firmly.

ASSERTIVE DISCIPLINE PLAN

Through Assertive Discipline we will present you with the specific skills you need to overcome these roadblocks and let your children know what it is you want them to do—and how to make sure they do it!

We will begin our discussion by helping you understand where you are having trouble with your children's behavior. Then we will give you a step-by-step plan to help guide your efforts.

Step 1: Communicate assertively. You will be taught how to speak so that your children will listen. You will learn how to avoid arguing with your children, as well as how to praise them when they behave.

Step 2: Back up your words with actions. For some children actions do speak louder than words. For those children you will learn how to quickly plan how you will respond if they do or do not listen to you when you have assertively communicated with them.

Step 3: Lay down the law. Finally, you will be taught how to systematically respond to your children's misbehavior when all else has failed. You will be taught techniques and skills to utilize with the most difficult situations.

Through the Assertive Discipline Plan we are going to show you how you can get your children to listen to you. You will no longer have to live with the frustration, anxiety and anger that parents feel when they believe they have little or no control over their children's disruptive, defiant or destructive behavior. You will no longer have to assault children—verbally or physically—in a vain attempt at parental control.

Please Note: Assertive Discipline was designed for all parents who want to develop better skills in dealing with their children's behavior. The goal of Assertive Discipline is to help parents take charge before the problems with their children get out of hand. This book was not written for parents of teenagers who are incorrigible or who have drug problems. Assertive Discipline can help those parents, but it should not be used as a substitute for professional counseling or specialized parent-support groups.

Finally, changing how you respond to your children is not easy, and please don't take anything we have written to even hint that it is so. We are well aware, from our own experiences, that for many reasons we fall into habits of responding in one way or another to our children. No one simply reads a book, "sees the light," and changes like magic. Since we know how hard it is to change habits, we have structured this book to provide you with as much support and guidance as we can.

Chapter 2 INEFFECTIVE RESPONSES

Before you can begin to change how you deal with your children's misbehavior, it is important to recognize how you currently respond when your children don't listen to you.

In our studies we found that most parents are unaware of how ineffectively they react when their children misbehave. They don't realize that their manner of responding may often encourage their children to continue to misbehave. We have broken down ineffective responses into two categories: *nonassertive* and *hostile.*

If you are like most parents, some of the following responses will sound familiar to you.

NONASSERTIVE RESPONSES

Nonassertive responses are ineffective because the parents are not clearly stating what they want to their children or, if they are, they are not prepared to back up their words with action. When parents respond in a nonassertive manner, they allow their children to take advantage of them because they communicate to the children that they do not mean business.

We want to help you understand why nonassertive responses tend to be ineffective. Here are examples of typical nonassertive responses parents may make to their children's misbehavior and why the responses do not work.

Statement of Fact: "You're Still Not Doing What I Want." Many parents feel that it is useful to point out to their children that they are misbehaving.

> **Child:** (Again does not do what parent told him to.)
> **Parent** (frustrated): You are still not listening to me!

This response assumes your children are not aware of what they are doing and that if they were, they would stop their misbehavior. Unfortunately, most children are fully aware that they are doing something you do not want them to do, and telling them what they are doing does not communicate what you really want, which is for them to stop. This response is frequently followed by questions.

Questions: "Why Are You Doing That?" Most of today's parents feel that if they can determine the cause of their children's misbehavior, they can stop it. In theory this principle is sound; in practice it rarely works. Most young children do not know why they are misbehaving and most older children give you reasons you probably will not like.

> **Parent:** Why don't you listen to me?
> **Young child:** I don't know.
> **Parent:** Well, what's wrong?
> **Young child:** Nothing.

> **Parent:** Why don't you listen to me?
> **Older child:** I don't want to.
> **Parent:** Why?
> **Older child:** I want to do things my way.

Parents may also respond to their children's misbehavior with other types of ineffective questions.

> **Child** (about to walk out the door without cleaning up toys and clothes): See you later, Mom.

Parent (frustrated): How many times do I have to talk to you about cleaning up after yourself?

(What does that parent want the child to say? Six times? Seven times?)

Child: I'm sorry I broke another window.
Parent (wringing hands): What am I going to do with you?

Why should the child listen to a parent if the parent is asking the child how he or she should be dealt with?

TIP   Children learn to tune you out when you are nonassertive.

Beg and Plead: "Please Try to Behave!" Many parents feel so overwhelmed they end up pleading with their children to behave.

Child: I don't want to go to bed.
Parent: It's ten o'clock. I can't take any more noise. Please try to go to bed. Okay?
Child: No, I'm not tired.
Parent: But I am. Please, go to sleep so I can get some rest.

When parents plead, they are asking their child to feel sorry for them. That is usually not enough of a reason for a disruptive child to behave.

Demand the Children Behave, But Do Not Follow Through: "I Told You to Do What I Say." Not following through is a classic, nonassertive response to misbehavior. The parent responds with a firm demand, yet does nothing to make the child comply if the child does not want to.

Parent: Susan, stop watching television and get your chores done right now! I'm tired of having to talk to you about this.

Child: Okay, Dad. I'll do them.

A few minutes later her parent returns; child is still watching television.

Parent: Susan, I told you to do your chores. Now turn off that TV and do them.

Child: You're right, Dad. I'll do them.

Parent again returns in a few minutes; child is still watching television.

Parent: Doggone it, Susan. I told you to turn off that TV and do your chores! I've had it with you. You never listen to me!

TIP   When you threaten to discipline your children and do not follow through, you are teaching them not to listen to you.

Ignore the Problem: "There's Nothing I Can Do, So Why Try?" Some parents feel so inadequate attempting to deal with their children's misbehavior that they ignore it as though it had never occurred.

We observed a woman in a market with her two children who were repeatedly using "four-letter" words in their conversation. After some time the woman's friend turned to her in a perturbed manner and asked, "Don't you hear the words your kids are using?" The mother replied, "I don't pay any attention anymore. I've tried to stop them, but they just won't listen to me, so why bother?''

As you can see, nonassertive responses can range from indirect statements and firm demands that are not followed through on to just ignoring the behavior. What they all have in common is the lack of impact needed to communicate to your children that you do mean business.

HOSTILE RESPONSES

The second type of ineffective response is hostility. Hostile responses are those that parents make that are designed to get their children to behave, while disregarding the children's needs and feelings. When parents respond in this way their manner communicates to the children "I don't like you." Often when parents respond in a hostile manner, they are trying to get back at their children rather than to help them behave. Here are examples of typical hostile responses parents utilize.

Verbal Put-Downs: "You Make Me Sick." The parents respond to the misbehavior of their children with angry verbal assaults.

Parent (angrily): I got another bad note from your teacher. You're just impossible. I've never seen a kid act as bad as you do. I'm sick of you and your lousy attitude!

TIP   Hostile responses usually result in negative feelings between you and your children.

Unrealistic Threats: "You're Going to Get It!" Many parents when they are frustrated threaten their children with punishment "if" the children continue misbehaving.

"If you act up at school one more time, you've had it!"
"If you ever talk to me like that again I'm going to
beat you within an inch of your life."

Threats may sound strong, but we have found that most children learn at an early age that phrases such as "if you do that again, I'm going to . . ." are *not* usually enforced by the parents. The children learn to disregard such messages and continue their misbehavior.

TIP   The louder you yell, the less
effective you will be. Hostile screaming
and yelling communicate to your children
you are out of control.

Severe Punishment: "You Can't Leave Your Room for a Week." When children misbehave they are punished, often severely. The punishment may be anything the parents feel the children do not want to happen. Often the punishment is designed more for parents to release their frustration than as a corrective action for the children.

Two parents, Jane and Ralph, reported this to us: Their thirteen-year-old son would periodically leave the house and not tell them he was going. One day he was gone for a particularly long time and when he returned they exploded. Angrily, they grounded him in the house for "one whole month."

Jane told us that by the end of a few days, "I couldn't handle having him around for one more minute. His being stuck in the house was worse for me than it was for him." The parents felt they had to back down from their overly severe punishment and let him go outside.

Physical Response: "I'm Going to Give You What You Deserve." We have worked with parents who have used such responses as pulling the children's hair, squeezing their arms, throwing them against the wall, or beating them. These responses meet only the parents' need to release their anger and hurt and do not help set up limits for their children.

Just as children learn that their parents do not mean business when they utilize indirect, nonassertive responses, the children learn the same thing regarding the parents' hostile responses. They know that your loud threats and inappropriate punishment are indications that you probably feel that you cannot get them to behave or are not willing to put forth the effort necessary to make them toe the line. Thus your children continue to challenge and battle with you.

POINTS TO REMEMBER:
INEFFECTIVE RESPONSES

When your children misbehave, avoid nonassertive responses such as:

Questions: Why don't you listen to me?
How many times do I have to talk to you?
What am I going to do with you?

Begging: Please try to behave.

Threatening: Next time you do that, you're in trouble. (Yet failing to follow through when the child does misbehave.)

When your children misbehave, avoid hostile responses such as:

Verbal put-downs: You are a terrible child.

Unrealistic threats: If you do that again you will wish you didn't live here!

Overly severe punishment: You can't ever have a friend over again.

Physical responses that release your anger.

Chapter 3 STEP 1: COMMUNICATE ASSERTIVELY

Now that you are aware of the ineffective ways in which you respond to your children's misbehavior, you are ready to learn a new, more effective approach—Assertive Discipline.

As we said before, Assertive Discipline is a three-step program. You should begin with Step One, and then if the severity of your children's misbehavior warrants it, continue to Steps Two and Three.

The first step of Assertive Discipline is to speak so that your children will listen. In order to do that, you will need to assume a more assertive manner. When you are assertive, you clearly and firmly communicate to your children that what you say is what you mean. To respond in a more assertive, take-charge manner, you will need to acquire these four communication skills:

- How to speak assertively
- How to use nonverbal messages
- How to handle arguing
- How to catch 'em being good

HOW TO SPEAK ASSERTIVELY

How should you speak to your children when their behavior is such a problem to you, themselves, or others that you feel the problem must stop? Through our years of professional and clinical experience we have found that when parents are determined that their children behave, they have addressed their children with direct, assertive statements:

I want you to get dressed for school now!
Get your homework done immediately!
You will not tease your sister!

Such direct, assertive messages leave no doubt in your children's minds exactly what you want them to do. This way of speaking is critical when you want your children to listen to you.

TIP   **When speaking assertively, be specific: Avoid vague statements such as "act nice," "be good," or "act your age."**

Here are further examples of what we mean: It is fifteen minutes before dinner and you walk into your seven-year-old's room. It is cluttered with toys.

Parent: John, why don't you start cleaning up your room. Dinner is almost ready.

Child (continues to play): I don't like cleaning my room.

Parent (walks over to the child, looks him straight in the eye and calmly and firmly says): *I understand, but I want you to put these toys away right now!*

Or it's 8:00 P.M. You're sitting in the living room reading the newspaper. Your daughter is in her room talking on the telephone.

Parent (calling to daughter): It's getting late. Have you finished your homework yet?

Daughter (calls back): No. I'm still talking to my friend.

Parent (walks calmly into daughter's room, sits down on the bed next to her, looks her straight in the eye): *Ellen, I want you to hang up the phone and do your homework immediately!*

HOW TO USE NONVERBAL TECHNIQUES

Just as important as what you say to your children is how you say it. To maximize the impact of your words, here are some points to follow:

Stay calm. Don't scream or yell your requests at your children. Speak in a firm, calm tone of voice. By staying calm, you will communicate to your children that you are in control.

Look your children in the eye when you speak. Eye contact is vital to human communication. We say as much with our eyes as with our words. You can increase the effectiveness of any message to your children by looking them in the eye when you speak.

> TIP   If your child will not look at you, gently turn his or her head until your eyes meet.

Gesture to add emphasis to your words. Hand gestures can often communicate nonverbally to the child, "I mean what I'm saying." An important point to remember is that there is a major difference between a hand gesture designed to emphasize your words and one used to intimidate your child. We refer especially to shaking your finger in your child's face as you speak. This does little more than frighten the child.

Touch the child. Touch adds the impact of creating physical as well as verbal limits. Placing your hand on your child as you speak is a clear indicator of the sincerity and forcefulness of your message. For some children your hand on their shoulder will communicate more than words can say.

HOW TO HANDLE ARGUING: THE "BROKEN RECORD" TECHNIQUE

Many times when you try to tell your children what you want, all you get is an argument. For example:

Parent: Seth, will you please pick up your toys? They're all over the family room.

Seth: Why do I always have to clean up? Brian never does.

Parent: What do you mean? You always leave your things out—he doesn't.

Seth (getting upset): You always pick on me.

Parent (getting agitated): That's not true.

Seth: You're not fair.

Parent (upset): What are you saying? I think I'm fair. Oh, I give up!

The parent in this example ended up wondering whether she was "fair" rather than just continuing to state what she wanted, which was for Seth to pick up his toys.

TIP   Always keep this in mind: You can never win an argument with a child.

We have found a useful means to help you stick to your point and avoid fruitless arguments with your children. We call it the *broken record*. It gets its name because when you use it, you sound like a broken record that keeps repeating the same thing over and over. When you learn to speak as if you were a broken record, you will be capable of expressing your wants and needs and will be able to ignore the side-tracking efforts of your children. Getting back to Seth:

Parent: Seth, will you please pick up your toys? [Statement of want] They are all over the family room.

Seth: Why do I always have to clean up? Brian never does.

Parent (calmly): That's not the point. *I want you to pick up your toys.* [Broken record]

Seth: You always pick on me!

Parent (calmly): That's not the point. *I want you to pick up your toys.* [Broken record]

Seth (calming down): All right. I hear you. I'll do it.

Here are some simple guidelines for using the broken record when your children argue with you.

1. Determine what you want your child to do. "I want you to pick up your toys."
2. Keep repeating what you want when your child argues with you. Do not respond to any statement from the child.
3. Use a broken record a maximum of three times. If your child still does not do what you want, be prepared to back up your words with actions (as we will discuss in Step Two). Here's what we mean:

Parent (with eye contact, hand on shoulder): Ken, you will stop bothering your brother. [Statement of want]

Ken: It's not my fault. He picks on me.

Parent (firmly): That's not the point. *You will stop bothering your brother.* [Broken record]

Ken: You're just picking on me. I'll do what I want!
Parent (calmly): Ken, *you will stop bothering your brother.* [Broken record] *You have a choice: You will leave him alone or you will be grounded until bedtime.*
Ken: Wow, you must hate me. You're on my case like everybody else.
Parent (calmly): Ken, if you bother your brother again you will be grounded until bedtime.

HOW TO CATCH 'EM BEING GOOD

As we just discussed, being assertive means clearly and firmly communicating what you want your children to do. Equally important is the ability to respond assertively when your children do listen to you.

The key to being assertive lies in balancing your disciplinary statements with frequent acknowledgment of your children's positive behavior.

Ask yourself this:

● You have had trouble with your child's talking back. How do you respond when he is cooperative?
● Your children continually argue and fight with each other. How do you respond when they play quietly?
● Your child is a constant problem at school. How do you respond when you get a good report from her teacher?

Unfortunately, many parents do not take charge and respond in an assertive ''I-like-that'' manner when their children do behave. They do not realize their children's emotional well-being and self-confidence are directly related to the feedback they receive from their parents.

Therefore, when your children behave, you must be prepared to reinforce their behavior. By reinforce, we mean responding in a manner that, through your words and actions, demonstrates your approval and appreciation of your child's behavior. The more positive your responses, the better your children will feel and behave.

One of the best ways to communicate your love and concern to your children is to permeate your relationship with your positive feedback. Don't take their "good" behavior for granted. Let your children know how much you appreciate it when they behave.

> TIP **Keep in mind children need your attention. If they do not feel they can get it when they are good, they will attempt to get it by misbehaving.**

Use any or all of the following approaches to reinforce your children's positive behavior.

Praise: Effective parents are aware of the enormous impact their praise can have and will utilize it not only to build their children's self-esteem, but to help them learn appropriate behavior. Praise is the most useful, positive reinforcer you possess.

I like how cooperative you are today.
You sure did a great job getting ready for school.
I'm proud of how hard you worked on your school assignment.
You did a terrific job cleaning up your room.

When praising your children, keep the following guidelines in mind:

1. Tell them, specifically, what they are doing, or have done, that you like. "I really do appreciate how quietly you are sitting in the back seat, Natalie," rather than making a vague comment such as, "You are a good girl, Natalie."
2. When you deliver your verbal praise, be sure to walk up to your children, look them in the eye, and, if appropriate, give them a gentle pat on the shoulder in order to increase the impact of your message.
3. When you praise your children, watch out for hostile, sarcastic comments. The quickest way to turn your children off is to couple your positive comments with negative "hooks": "I like the way you cleaned up today. It's about time." "Thank you for helping your sister. I expect you to do the same tomorrow." "You were so good today. I sure like it, but I can't believe you acted so nice." These "digs" are poorly veiled hostilities on the part of frustrated parents.

"Super Praise": "Super praise" is one of the most powerful tools you can use to let your children know that you like it when they behave. Here's how to do it:

First, you praise your child for behaving.

Mother (to child): You have been so helpful around the house today. I want to make sure Dad knows about this when he comes home.

Second, you praise your child in front of another adult.

Mother (to father in child's presence): I had such a nice day with Jamie. I am so proud of the way she cooperated today.

Third, the other adult praises the child.

Father (to child): I really like getting such good reports from Mom about you. You really are special. [Father hugs child]

Nonverbal Praise: Hand-in-hand with verbal praise go nonverbal responses. A hug can mean as much or more than countless "I like that's." A smile, a wink, a pat on the shoulder—all communicate your positive support and recognition of your children's appropriate behavior.

TIP   Make it a habit to praise each child at least three times a day.

TIP   If your child is having a particularly difficult day, find something that was done right and tell your child how much you liked it.

PULLING IT ALL TOGETHER

What we are saying in Step One is that when your children misbehave you need to give them a firm, clear, assertive message that you want the behavior to stop, and your verbal limits must at all times be balanced by frequent praise when your children do what you want. Here's how it's done.

Parent (walking up to child and looking him in the eye): Adam, it is not time to watch TV. I want you to get ready for school right now!" [Assertive statement]

Child: But I just want to watch for a few more minutes.

Parent (calmly): I understand, but I want you to get ready for school right away. [Broken record]

Child: Oh, come on, please. . . .

Parent (calmly): I want you to get ready right away. [Broken record]

Child: Oh, all right. I hear you.

The next morning the parent observes the child getting ready for school on time.

Parent: I'm sure proud of how you are getting ready by yourself. [Positive statement]

Create a balance. When the child misbehaves, set limits; when the child behaves, provide praise.

POINTS TO REMEMBER:
COMMUNICATING ASSERTIVELY

- Make assertive statements: "I want you to listen to me."

- Stay calm. Don't yell at your children.

- When you speak, make eye contact, gesture, touch your children.

- Avoid arguing with your children; keep repeating what you want.

- Use the "broken record."

Parent:	I want you to clean up the yard.
Child:	Why me? Everyone else is playing.
Parent:	I understand. But I want you to clean up the yard.

- When children do what you want, catch them being good and praise them: "I like how you got ready for school."

- Use "super praise."

Father:	Great job on your spelling test. We've got to show Mom.
Father	(to mother): Take a look at how great Josh did on his spelling.
Mother	(to child): I'm so proud of how hard you worked on your spelling.

- Give hugs or other nonverbal support when children behave.

Chapter 4　STEP 2: BACK UP YOUR WORDS WITH ACTIONS

In the first step of Assertive Discipline we discussed how to communicate assertively. Now, we know what some of you are thinking: "At times no matter what I say, or how I say it, my children will not do what I want. They ignore my wishes and continue to misbehave." If this is the case, it is time for you to implement Step Two and back up your words with actions.

For many children, "Actions speak louder than words." In order to assert your influence effectively, often it is necessary to demonstrate your sincerity by reinforcing your verbal requests with appropriate actions. Your actions will take the form of providing consequences, either negative or positive depending on the child's behavior. We are not advocating that you run around your house continually telling your children, "Do what I tell you to do or I will send you to your room." What we are saying is that you should determine consequences to use ahead of time, and when it is necessary and appropriate, back up your words with actions.

To effectively back up your words with actions, you must acquire three skills:

- How to use disciplinary consequences for inappropriate behavior
- How to handle "testing"
- How to provide positive support when you catch 'em being good

HOW TO USE DISCIPLINARY CONSEQUENCES

As soon as you have assertively told your children what you want them to do and anticipate that they may not comply, ask yourself this vital question: **"What will I do if they do not listen to me?"** In other words, there and then determine how you are going to back up your words with actions to ensure your children learn proper behavior. (Will you send them to their room? Take away TV privileges? etc.)

The key to this skill is thinking on your feet. Don't wait until your children misbehave again to decide how you will act. Prepare yourself immediately. The more prepared you are, the easier it will be for you to help your children stop their misbehavior.

The following guidelines will help you to quickly determine the consequences you can use if your children do not listen:

The Consequences Must Be Something That the Children Do Not Like But That Are Not Physically or Psychologically Harmful. Any disciplinary consequence, to be effective, must be something the children do not particularly enjoy. A four- or five-year-old probably will not enjoy being sent to his or her room for five or ten minutes, but typical twelve- or thirteen-year-olds would probably not mind being sent to their rooms, where they would be able to entertain themselves with TV, radio, or cassette players.

While the disciplinary consequences you select should not be enjoyable to children, the consequences also should not degrade them either physically or emotionally.

The most common disciplinary consequences parents utilize successfully include the following:

Separation: The children are separated from you and others into a nonstimulating, "boring" situation such as standing or sitting in the corner, going to their rooms, the guest room, or sitting on the porch.

TIP   Set a kitchen timer so the children will know when the time they must spend in their rooms or the corner, etc., is finished.

TIP   If you find your children do not mind going to their own room to be disciplined, you may want to remove their favorite toys, games, TV, or phone to ensure the experience is boring, not enjoyable.

Taking away privileges: You suspend the child's privilege to watch TV, play outside, use the telephone, eat snacks, etc.

"Do what I want first": You make your children comply with your request before they can do something they want. "You cannot go outside and play until you clean up."

Grounding: You restrict your children to their yard, house, or room for a specific amount of time.

Physical action: You respond to younger children by holding them, physically making them do what you want.

In Appendix 1 we will provide detailed descriptions of various types of disciplinary consequences you may find useful in planning how to deal with your children.

Whenever Possible, the Consequences Should Be Logically Related to the Misbehavior. You will teach your children appropriate behavior more quickly when the disciplinary consequences you use are logically related to the misbehavior. For example:

Behavior Problem	Logical Consequence
Your ten-year-old damages your tools.	He is not allowed to use your tools for two weeks.
Your fourteen-year-old continually plays the stereo too loudly in her room.	You take the stereo out of her room for one week.
Your nine-year-old willfully breaks his brother's toy.	He has to use his allowance to buy his brother another toy.
Your five-year-old splashes water and makes a mess in the bathroom when taking a bath.	She is required to clean up bathroom.

Consequences Should Be Provided as a Choice. An integral part of backing up your words with actions is to provide your children with a choice. Your limit-setting consequences need to be spelled out to your children so that they can make the choice as to whether or not the consequences will occur.

Parent: Aaron, I cannot allow you to bother your brother at the dinner table. If you poke or hit your brother one

more time you will choose to sit in your room. It's
your choice.

Aaron: Okay. [However, he gradually begins to poke his
brother under the table.]

Parent: Aaron, you poked your brother; you have chosen to
go sit in your room for the remainder of dinner.

When you provide your children with the choice as to
whether or not the disciplinary consequences will occur, you
place the responsibility where it belongs—on the children.
The child is the one who chooses to poke his brother; thus,
he is the one who chooses to go to his room. When you give
your children choices, you are providing them with the op-
portunity to learn the natural consequences of their actions
and that they are responsible for their behavior.

**The Consequence Should Be Provided as Soon as Possible After the Child
Chooses Not to Listen to You.** When your children do not
listen to you, immediately notify them of the disciplinary
consequences. You may enforce the consequence at that
time:

Parent: Ryan, it is not time to watch TV. It is time to do the
dishes.

Child: Come on, Mom.

Parent: Ryan, you know the rule. There will be no TV until
the dishes are done.

On the other hand, you may inform the children of a consequence that will occur in the future:

Child (again arrives home after not telling her parent where
she would be): Hi, Dad.

Parent (sits down with child): Kathy, I told you that I'm not
comfortable with your going out without letting me
know where you'll be. I told you that if you did so
again, you would choose to be grounded.

Child: But, Dad, I'm really sorry.

Parent: No buts, Kathy. I have to know where you are going. I'm sorry you didn't listen to me. You chose to be grounded tomorrow afternoon.

Provide the Consequence Every Time the Child Chooses to Misbehave. Consistency is the key to backing up your words with actions. No disciplinary consequence will work unless your children know it will occur on a regular basis.

Child: [Constantly gets wild when family is trying to watch TV.]

Parent: Mike, you're annoying all of us again. As I told you, you have chosen to stay in your room until you can calm down.

Child: [Goes to room and comes out ten minutes later and quickly starts to play wildly.]

Parent: Mike, I can't allow you to disturb us when we're watching TV. You will choose to stay in your room every time you can't control yourself. Please go to your room and stay there fifteen minutes.

Provide the Consequence in a Matter-of-Fact, Nonhostile Manner. Many children get a real thrill out of getting their parents worked up into a frenzy. In such cases, it may be worth it to the child to be grounded, to miss TV, or to miss a privilege just to see you ranting and raving. To discipline children effectively, please be calm.

Child (angrily): I don't have to listen to you!

Parent (in a calm, firm manner): Jay, I told you I cannot allow you to talk to me that way. You have chosen to stay in your room until you are ready to talk to me in a nice manner. Please, go to your room now!

TIP   Never take a consequence away. If
you back down, your children will never
learn you mean business.

If Your Disciplinary Consequence Does Not Work, Change It. Speaking realistically, disciplinary consequences are not effective with some children no matter how consistently they are used. If you have consistently utilized a disciplinary consequence and it is clear that your children's behavior has not improved, we recommend you select a different consequence. Here is an example:

Parent: Jeremy, I want you to stop making so much racket with your toys. We cannot hear the stereo with all the noise you are making. If you continue to make noise, I will have to take the toys away from you.

Jeremy: Okay, Dad. [After a few minutes he begins to fire his laser pistol, which makes a tremendous racket.]

Parent: Jeremy, that pistol makes too much noise. I have to take it away from you. Please give it to me.

Jeremy: Okay, Dad, here's the pistol. I'm sorry I made too much noise with it. [Within ten minutes Jeremy is playing with a motorized truck, which again distracts the entire family.]

Parent: Jeremy, that truck makes too much noise. Now I told you I want you to play quietly with some toys like your blocks.

Jeremy: [Takes out his blocks and plays quietly for a couple of minutes, but then begins smashing them loudly.]

Parent: Jeremy, stop making all that noise with those blocks. Give me those blocks now.

Even though his parents consistently followed through and took his toys away, Jeremy continued to make noise. It then became necessary for his parents to utilize a different consequence.

Parent: Jeremy, you have a choice: Either you play quietly in the family room with your toys, or you have to go outside to play.

Forgive and Forget. Once your child has received the consequence he or she has chosen, the issue is over and it is time to move on. Do not harbor any anger or resentment. Instead, let your child know you have confidence in your child's ability to improve his or her behavior.

Parent (enters child's room): The twenty minutes are up. Your grounding is over. I really don't like keeping you in your room, but it's my job as your parent to help teach you how to behave.

Child: I know. It's just that sometimes it's so hard for me to control myself.

Parent: I understand, and I'm confident you will learn how. Most important, don't forget that I'm on your side, and you will always be my favorite little person. [Hugs child]

HOW TO HANDLE "TESTING"

When you discipline your children for their misbehavior, watch out—they will often test you to see if you really mean business. Children most frequently test parents by crying or by being defiant. Notice how the child in the following example uses tears to test his father:

Parent (observing his son roughly shoving another child): David, I told you that if you shove the other children you have to go home. Now let's go, young man!

Child (immediately starts to cry): I'm sorry. I won't do it again. Please give me another chance.

Parent: David, I can't. You must learn a lesson.

Child (begins to sob loudly): Please! Just one more chance!

Parent (becoming concerned about how upset his son is): David, it's O.K. Just calm down. Please stop crying. It's not that big of a deal to get so upset about, dear.

Child (continues to sob): But I want to stay in the park.

Parent (becoming concerned): O.K. Just stop crying. I can't take it.

Older children may become defiant when you discipline them, as in this situation:

Child (angrily): Forget it! I'm not doing the dishes tonight!

Parent (firmly): Cathy, I told you if you do not cooperate, you have to go to your room for thirty minutes. Now, go!

Child (fuming): I'm not going!

Parent (getting angry): Yes, you will! [Parent escorts child to room]

Child (five minutes later she leaves the room): I won't stay in my room. You're unfair!

Parent (becoming agitated): What do you mean? I told you to stay there. I'm sick and tired of your carrying on.

Child (yelling): You started it!

Parent (throwing up hands in disgust): Just leave me alone. Do what you want. You don't listen to anything I say!

Parents who back down when they are tested are in effect teaching their children the following lesson: If you get upset enough, or angry enough, you can get your way. Their children thus learn to continually have a tantrum or fight, knowing that eventually their parents will back down.

In order for you to stand your ground when your children test you, you need to respond assertively. Here's how the parents could have more effectively handled their children in the previous situations:

Parent (observing child roughly pushing another child): David, I told you that if you shoved the other children, you have to go home. Now let's go home, young man.

Child (immediately starting to cry): I'm sorry. I won't do it again. Please give me another chance.

Parent (calmly): David, I understand how upset you are, but you shoved, so you have to go home. [Broken record]

Child (sobbing): Please! Just one more chance!

Parent (firmly takes child by arm and begins to escort him out): David, I understand how upset you are. But you shoved your friend and you must go home now! [Broken record]

Child (becoming hysterical, throws himself on the ground): No!

Parent (firmly picks child up): David, you're leaving even if I have to carry you.

Child (angrily): Forget it. I'm not doing the dishes!

Parent (calmly): Cathy, I told you if you do not cooperate, you will have to stay in your room for thirty minutes. Now go!

Child (fuming): I'm not going!

Parent (calmly): Yes you will! [Parent escorts child to her room]

Child (leaves room after five minutes): I won't stay in my room any longer. You are unfair.

Parent (firmly escorting child back to room): Cathy, go back to your room. If you come out again you will stay twice as long.

Child (angrily comes right out of room): I'm not staying. . . .

Parent (looking child in the eye and stating firmly): Cathy, you will stay in your room for one hour. If you choose to come out again, you will stay for two hours. I'm the boss, not you!

TIP   It helps to anticipate at what times your children will test you. Let them know that you are prepared to stand your ground. "You will go to your room and you will stay there no matter how long you cry."

TIP   When your children test you, stay calm, speak assertively, and if they argue, use the "broken record."

The "I-Don't-Care" Child: There is one other type of "testing" that children engage in when you set limits. This differs from the highly emotional variety we have just discussed and in many ways is more difficult for parents to handle. We call this testing "I-don't-care." Here's how children use this manipulation: When you tell your children they must behave and you promise to discipline them if they don't, they typically respond with a "So what—who cares?" Such a blasé response is difficult to deal with, since you are probably accustomed to your children giving you a frightened, upset, or distressed look when you tell them you will send them to their room, take away TV, or ground them.

If you are like most parents, when your child says to you, "So what, I don't care if you do that," you experience a sinking feeling and say to yourself, "What am I going to do? Nothing works with that child!" *Not true!* "I-don't-care" children are manipulating you. They have learned that this kind of response often sidetracks their parents from dealing with them effectively. "I-don't-care" children do not require a broken-record response; they need you to do as these parents did.

Parent: Beth, you need to do your homework. You simply cannot talk on the phone or watch TV until it's done.

Child: So? I don't care.

Parent: It's your choice then—no TV and no phone.

Child: [Sits in room entire night and does not do any homework]
(Next night)

Parent: Beth, it's homework time. Your brother is doing his work and I want you to do yours.

Child: Yeah, I know. I just don't feel like doing it.

Parent: You know there's no TV or phone.

Child: Well, big deal. [Child sits again in room for entire night without doing homework]
(Next night)

Parent: Beth, the rule is still in effect: no homework—no TV or phone.

Child (getting upset): How long is this going to last?

Parent: Until you do your homework without any hassles.

Child: But tonight my favorite shows are on TV.

Parent: It's your choice, Beth. If you want to watch your shows, your homework must be done.

Child: Well, all right, I guess I'd better get it done. I'm going to get to work. I'll see you soon.

Parent: I'm really glad you're doing your work. Good job, dear!

There are few children who would not care if they knew they would not be allowed to watch TV, talk on the telephone, or play every day that their homework was not completed. There are few children who would not care if they knew you would take their toys away every time that they left them around the house, even if it meant that you would do this day in and day out.

If you really care, the children will really care. If you are prepared to use all means necessary and appropriate to influence the children to eliminate their disruptive and inappropriate behavior, they will sense your determination and begin to care about the consequences they will have to face if they choose to act inappropriately.

TIP   Use the same disciplinary consequence three times. If it doesn't work, try a "tougher" one.

How to Provide Positive Support When You Catch 'Em Being Good

As important as planning what you will do when your children don't listen to you is planning how you will respond when they do. The key to teaching your children to behave is again: *Catch 'em being good.*

In Step One we talked about the importance of praise in changing your children's behavior. However, with some children, especially of school age, praise alone may not be sufficient to motivate them to improve their behavior quickly. With those children it is advisable to combine your praise with additional motivators, whether they are special privileges or special rewards. For example:

Special privileges: Justin, you played so nicely with your brother, you may stay up one hour later.

Special rewards: Gail, you have been so cooperative, let's go to McDonald's for lunch.

We are aware that many parents are reluctant to reward their children with anything but praise because they are afraid that their children will become used to a pattern of behaving only if they get some reward. For example:

I will not clean up my room unless you promise to read a story.
What will you give me for doing the dishes?

Please don't forget that even when using rewards you are still the boss! Your children do not decide what rewards they will receive for behaving—you do. If your children want to get into a power struggle with you and try to extort rewards by threat of misbehavior, do not tolerate it.

Here are some guidelines for responding with positive support:

Your Response Must Be Something Your Children Want. Ask yourself, What would my children like to earn? For your positive response to motivate your children to continue the behavior you desire, the reward must be something they need or would like to have. Some children will "walk on water" simply for your praise. Other children desire sharing activities with you. Some would be motivated by a visit to a video arcade, some by staying out late at night.

If you are not sure which rewards would most motivate your children, see page 120 of Appendix 2 for a questionnaire to give them.

You Must Reinforce Your Children's Behavior Immediately. In order to maximize the impact of your positive response, you should make

the response as soon as possible after your children exhibit
the behavior you desire.

Praise:

> **Child** (does homework for first time with no hassles): Mom,
> my homework is done.
> **Parent:** Kevin, that's terrific. You got all of your homework
> done on your own. Great job!

Special Privilege:

> **Child** (gets ready for bed on time on his own): Dad, I'm
> ready for bed.
> **Parent:** Jess, I really appreciate your getting ready on your
> own. That is so neat. How about our reading an extra
> story from your favorite book?

TIP   For most young children extra
"special time" with you playing a game,
playing ball, etc., is the best privilege
they can earn.

Special Reward:

> **Children:** [Do not argue throughout dinner]
> **Parent:** Kids, great job getting along. You each may have
> your favorite dessert tonight.

Too many parents praise their children at night for the behavior that occurred in the morning or let them go to the park
because they behaved well earlier that week. Parents often
make the mistake of offering long-range rewards to children.
It is not fruitful to offer a new bike next summer to a seven-

year-old for good behavior at school. Many parents promise their young children a special toy at Christmas for good behavior during the fall. Realistically, most children do not have the maturity or the mental capacity to hold long-range goals in mind day after day.

You Should Consistently Reinforce Your Children When They Behave. When you begin to work with your children on improving their behavior, you will need to reinforce them: "I like the way . . ." "Good job," etc., every time they engage in the behavior you have requested. Just praising or rewarding them once or twice will not produce results. You should be prepared to praise and reward your children consistently for several days, a week or two, or even longer, depending upon the child and his or her behavior, to get results. For example:

The parents praised their four-year-old daughter every time she got dressed by herself for one full week.

The parents praised their eight-year-old son every time he played cooperatively with his sister for nine days, and rewarded him at the end of this time by allowing him to pick his favorite restaurant when the family went out to eat.

The parents praised their twelve-year-old son every night that he did his homework for two weeks, and as a special reward gave him extra money to go skating at the end of this time.

TIP   The more positive you are with your children, the less you will have to set limits.

PULLING IT ALL TOGETHER

What we are saying in Step Two is this: When speaking assertively isn't enough, you must quickly decide how you will back up your words with actions. Then when your children begin to behave, be ready to catch them being good. Here's what we mean:

Parent (walking up to child and looking him in the eye): Terry, I have told you twice today that I cannot allow you to constantly tease and be nasty to your friends. You now have a choice, either stop teasing or your friends have to go home.

Child (getting upset): I don't want them to go home. I'm not doing anything!

Parent (calmly): It's your choice. Stop teasing or they will go home. [Broken record]

Child: [Stomps away and ten minutes later starts calling the other children names]

Parent: Terry, you are teasing your friends. You have chosen that they go home. I'm sure you can get along better tomorrow.

Next day, parent observes child playing nicely with his friends.

Parent: Terry, you are playing so nicely with your friends. How would all of you like some ice cream?

Remember, create a balance. Set firm limits; balance with positive support.

POINTS TO REMEMBER
BACK UP YOUR WORDS WITH ACTIONS

- For many children, actions speak louder than words.

- Quickly plan how you will back up your words with actions. As soon as you tell your children what you want them to do, ask yourself this: What do I do if they don't listen?

- Decide on a disciplinary consequence that will be effective. Give the child a choice: "If you do that, you will choose to be disciplined." Be consistent: Provide the consequence every time the child misbehaves. Forgive and forget: After the child has been disciplined, the issue is over.

- When you discipline your children, stand your ground if they test you. Don't back down if they cry, yell, etc.

- Plan how you will catch them being good. The key to teaching children to behave is to support their positive behavior. Use praise, special privileges, rewards.

- Create a balance. Set firm limits *and* catch 'em being good.

Chapter 5 STEP 3: LAY DOWN THE LAW

Through assertively communicating and backing up your words with actions you will be able to help your children change the vast majority of their problem behaviors. However, there are going to be times when you and your children have had such conflicts that you will need to move to Step Three and "lay down the law."

In order to lay down the law you must learn three skills:

- Set up a systematic Assertive Discipline Plan
- Use "parent-saver" techniques when all else fails
- Conduct a "lay-down-the-law" session with your children

SET UP A SYSTEMATIC ASSERTIVE DISCIPLINE PLAN

In the previous chapter we discussed how to come up with a "quick" discipline plan to help you respond more effectively to your children's everyday behavior problems.

Now we want to discuss how to develop a systematic Assertive Discipline Plan for more difficult problems.

A systematic plan is a written plan that you and your spouse develop together. It includes the behaviors you want your children to change, the consequences you will provide for misbehavior, the reinforcement you will use for positive behavior and how you will monitor your children's actions.

Why is such a systematic plan needed? When you reach a point with your children's behavior where nothing has worked to improve it, you may be feeling frustrated, over-whelmed, and at a loss for what to do next. Your children have given you a clear message: "I don't want to do what you want me to do!" You will begin to wonder if there is something wrong with your children, or perhaps even your-self, that has caused you to be so ineffective. In other words, you have probably lacked the necessary confidence to dem-onstrate to your children that you mean business and you are the boss.

A systematic Discipline Plan is a confidence builder. We say this for the following reasons. When you have a systematic plan for responding to your children's misbehavior, you are prepared. The more prepared you are the easier it will be for you to respond in a consistently assertive manner to your children's misbehavior. In order for you to get your children to stop their chronic misbehavior, you will have to respond more consistently than you normally do. This systematic plan will prove to be a vital asset in your efforts to take charge.

Here are the guidelines to follow to successfully establish a systematic Discipline Plan.

You and Your Spouse Should Develop the Plan Together. You and your spouse must work as a team if you want to teach your chil-dren to improve their chronic problem behaviors. Without teamwork your children will play the old "divide and con-quer" game.

TIP   Be sure to set aside at least twenty minutes of undisturbed time (i.e., no children, no TV, etc.) to develop a plan with your spouse.

Please Note: Single parents can get the same results by following the rest of the guidelines we will present.

Decide Which Behaviors You Want Your Children to Change. Give careful thought to which behaviors your children must change. Make a list of these specific behaviors. Then pick one or, at most, two behaviors per child that you and your spouse want them to change. (See worksheet on page 119 in Appendix 2.)

You and Your Spouse Must Decide How You Will Set Limits. Just as you and your spouse have to agree on the behaviors you want your children to change, you must agree as well on the disciplinary consequences that will be utilized. What are you both going to do if your children do not behave?

Decide if You Need to Monitor Your Children's Behavior. Many of your children's chronic problem behaviors can and will occur when you are not present. The children may act up at school, with a sitter, at a neighbor's or when they are at home alone. You cannot be truly consistent in your efforts unless you plan ways to monitor your children's behavior in order to discipline them if they misbehave even when you are not present. Here are some typical examples of how parents have successfully monitored the behavior of their children.

Telephone Calls: Call on a regular basis to check up on the children's behavior.

Your nine-year-old is constantly a severe problem in class. You call the teacher or have the teacher call you on a daily basis to report on your child's behavior.

Your six-year-old refuses to go to bed when the sitter tells her to. You call at bedtime and check up on her.

Your fourteen-year-old says she is going to a party at a friend's and that the friend's parents will chaperon. You call the parents to be sure one or both will be there.

Neighbor's Visits: Have a trusted neighbor stop by and check on your children when you are not home.

Your children do not do their homework when they are home alone. You have your neighbor come over to make sure it is done.

Your children become wild when they stay with the sitter. You have your neighbor stop by periodically to make sure the children are behaving.

Tape Recordings: You record the behavior of your children on tape so, if necessary, you can hear how they behaved while you were away. This is particularly effective if your children deny that they misbehave when you have been told they do.

Your thirteen-year-old talks back to his math teacher. You have the teacher record the entire class period.

Your seven-year-old will not listen to the babysitter. You have the sitter tape-record their interactions.

Written Notes: You have your children's teachers report to you in writing on their behavior.

Your ten-year-old does not do his homework. You have the teacher send you a note each day on the work that he must finish at home.

By monitoring their behavior you will demonstrate to your children your determination to teach them more appropriate behavior. You will show that you care about how they behave, not only when they are with you but when they are alone or with others.

Decide How You Will Both Catch Your Children Being Good. What will you and your spouse do when your children do what you want? In other words, how will you support their positive behavior? Will you praise them, provide them with privileges, provide them with awards? Use the worksheets in Appendix 2, page 120, to help you and your spouse set up a Discipline Plan.

TIP   Negative consequences may stop inappropriate behavior, but only positive reinforcement will change it.

USE "PARENT-SAVER" TECHNIQUES WHEN ALL ELSE FAILS

Here are some proven "parent-saver" ideas. You should consider including these ideas in your Discipline Plan.

Discipline Hierarchy: A Discipline Hierarchy is a particularly effective approach to use if your children engage in the same misbehavior many times per day. In a Discipline Hierarchy, your disciplinary consequences are ranked in order of severity. If your children continue to misbehave, they will receive increasingly severe consequences. For example:

First time your child does not cooperate: Warning that he or she will be disciplined the next time.
Second time your child does not cooperate: Fifteen minutes in his or her room.
Third time your child does not cooperate: Thirty minutes in his or her room.
Fourth time your child does not cooperate: One hour in his or her room.

The Discipline Hierarchy should be simple. It should contain a maximum of three or four consequences. The hierarchy should begin with a minor consequence such as a warning and progress in severity to more serious consequences such as grounding in the child's room for an extended period of time.

Most parents find it useful to keep track of their children's misbehavior by recording each disruption on a piece of paper or a small chalkboard or bulletin board placed in a strategic location like the kitchen. The first time the child misbehaves the parents write the child's name down as a warning. The next time the child breaks a rule the parent calmly puts a check, red mark, etc., next to the child's name, which indicates that the next consequence will be provided. Each subsequent misbehavior earns an additional check. This record-keeping enables you to be aware at all times of the consequences that your child has earned and of what consequences will next be provided for the child.

In addition, each day your child starts out with a clean slate. That means no matter how many times your children disrupted the previous day, they begin with the first consequence on your plan the first time they disrupt the next day. It is not beneficial to punish your children on Wednesday for the accumulated behavior problems that occurred on Tuesday.

One last point on the Discipline Hierarchy: We do not want you to interpret anything we have said to mean that you must utilize a Discipline Hierarchy. We want to state again that a Discipline Hierarchy may prove useful to you if your children consistently engage in the same misbehavior many times per day.

Positive Contract: A Positive Contract is basically an agreement between you and your children that states: "When you do what I want, in return I will provide you with something you want."

When you do your chores, I will give you an allowance.
When you spend all day without arguing or talking back, I will give you a point. When you have five points you and I will do a project in my workshop.

A Positive Contract is a helpful way to structure your reinforcement and positive support. Here are some basic guidelines on making and utilizing a Positive Contract with your children.

The contract must include what you want your child to do and what you will allow him or her to earn. You need to determine the specific behaviors you want to reinforce and what reward you will provide your children. Once again, a word of warning: Make sure the reward is not something that is too expensive or time-consuming to provide, such as a large toy or a trip.

The contract must be designed so that your children can earn the reward in an appropriate amount of time. The younger the child, the more quickly he or she needs to earn the consequence.

Three- to four-year-olds earn the reward within one day.
Five- to eight-year-olds earn the reward within one week.
Nine- to thirteen-year-olds earn the reward within two weeks.
Thirteen-year-olds and older earn the reward within four weeks.

TIP. **For older children, write the contract on paper, then both you and the child sign it.**

The contract should be in effect for a specific period of time. The contract should specify that the agreement will last for one week, two weeks, a month. When the time limit on the contract is over, determine if it would be helpful to draw up a new one. Decide if you want to change the consequences and ask the child if he or she wants something different as a reward. You will also want to decide if you want the child to engage in more positive behavior to earn the reward. For example, if it took ten points to earn time with you, maybe under this contract it would take fifteen or twenty points, or if the child needed to cooperate for one hour to earn a point, it would now take two hours.

To further assist you in developing a contract with your child or children, here are some examples of typical contracts parents have utilized:

Four-year-old who consistently interrupts his mom when she is on the phone.

For each time that I am on the phone and you do not interrupt me, you will earn a jellybean.

Seven-year-old who teases his sister.

For every hour that you spend without calling your sister a name, you will receive a chip. When you have twenty chips you and I will make a hand puppet.

Twelve-year-old who is a behavior problem at school
and who does not do her homework.

For every day that you follow directions in class and
do your homework without my having to tell you, you
will earn a point. When you earn ten points, you may
have extra money to go to the video arcade.

Let's go over what we have just discussed. A Positive Contract can be an excellent way to reinforce your children.
Contracts must be carefully planned to specify what you
want your children to do and what reward they can earn
quickly if they do comply.

Marble Mania: The second positive idea you may find useful is what we call
Marble Mania. This is designed to be utilized when you have
more than one child who is misbehaving. Marble Mania is the
most exciting, useful, and fun way we have ever found to
motivate children six years old and older to shape up. Here's
how Marble Mania works: When any of your children behave
as you have told them to, let them know you like it, and put
a marble in a jar: "Brandon, I really like how you have cooperated. You have earned a marble for that."

When the children fill the jar or reach a predetermined goal,
such as fifty, one hundred, or two hundred marbles, *all* the
children in the family earn the reward they want. The reward
may be the same for all the children, or each child may be
provided with a personalized reward. For example:

When you earn a hundred marbles, we will take all of
you to see a new science-fiction movie.

When you earn a hundred marbles, Emmy Lou will
get to go shopping for clothes with Mom, and Kris
will earn the right to go bowling with a friend.

In addition, the children should be provided with "bonus" marbles for each day they all go without misbehaving.

For each day that all of you go without misbehaving, we will put ten bonus marbles in the jar.

> TIP **To vary the method of tracking positive behavior, when the children are good you can put points, stars or stickers on a chart instead of marbles in a jar.**

The foundation of the tremendous success for a family reward system such as Marble Mania is the peer pressure that is fostered. By allowing all your children to earn something they want, they will be encouraged to motivate their siblings to be "good" in order to earn the reward as quickly as possible. You will hear the children imploring one another:

Stop bugging Mom! The less you carry on, the more marbles we will get, and the sooner we will both get what we want.

We have got to cut out our arguing. The less we fight, the more marbles Mom and Dad put in the jar. I don't know about you, but I want that prize!

Look, quit messing up! We can get ten extra marbles if we both go for the entire day without getting into trouble. So please, listen to Mom and the sitter!

Such peer pressure results in your children effectively motivating each other and consequently taking a great deal of pressure off you and your spouse.

Here are some guidelines to ensure the success of your Marble Mania plan. First, make sure your children earn a large number of marbles each day. Approximately once per hour to hour and a half, stop what you are doing and reward each child who has behaved as you have told him or her to by putting another marble in the jar. Be sure to let your children know what you are doing: "Steven, Bret, good job playing cooperatively. That's another marble for each of you."

If you need help remembering to reinforce your children, set your kitchen timer to ring in an hour or an hour and a half. When it rings give your children marbles if they have behaved.

Never remove marbles from the jar when the children misbehave. If the children have earned the marbles, they deserve to keep them.

At the end of each day, count the marbles in the jar and indicate the number to the children: "Kids, you have earned sixty-eight marbles. When you earn thirty-two more, you will have a hundred altogether and you will get your reward."

Many parents find it useful to use a Discipline Hierarchy and either a Positive Contract or Marble Mania when they establish a systematic Discipline Plan, which we will discuss next.

LAY DOWN THE LAW

Now it is time to put your systematic Discipline Plan into action. The first step is to meet with your children and lay down the law. In this no-nonsense talk you will need to reassert your parental authority in relation to your children's misbehavior. You must demand that your children change their problem behavior. You must send your children the following bottom-line message: "There is no way I am going to tolerate your misbehavior. You can behave, and I care too much about you to allow you to continue such problem behavior!" Here are the guidelines for a "Lay-Down-the-Law" session:

Meet with Your Child Only When Both of You Are Calm. To increase the probability that your child will listen to you, confront him or her when both of you are calm. Do not try to talk to your child right after a major fight, when your child or you are upset.

No Siblings Should Be Present When You Meet with the Child. If only one of your children misbehaved you do not need his or her sibling chiming in and making a scene during your discussion. (If you are having problems with two or more children you can meet with them at the same time.)

TIP   Make sure there will be no distractions when you meet with your child. Turn off the TV and stereo, take the phone off the hook, and tell your other children to stay out of the room so you will not be interrupted when you meet with your child.

Both Parents Should State Their Demand. In order to maximize the impact of the conversation, both parents should look the child in the eye and calmly and firmly state the demand to the child.

Mother: Brian, I am very concerned about your behavior. I cannot tolerate your wandering around the neighborhood and getting into trouble after school. You must come home right after school and do your homework and chores.

Father: I agree with your mom. You have gotten into too much trouble after school. You will come home right after school and get your schoolwork and chores done immediately.

State the Consequence That Will Occur if Your Child Chooses Not to Comply with Your Demands.* Clearly lay out what your child will choose to happen.

Father: Brian, If you do not come home straight from school and do your schoolwork and chores, you will be grounded for the remainder of the day at home with no television. And, Brian, if that does not work, we are prepared to ground you in your room for the entire day if you do not obey us!

Tell the Child How You Will Monitor His or Her Behavior. Your child must know you will, on a regular basis, check up to see if he or she is behaving appropriately, even when you are not present.

Mother: We will call you every day at 3:30 to see that you are home. When we get home from work, we will check to see that your chores and homework are finished. If you are not home when we call, or your work or chores are not done, you will be immediately grounded with no TV.

Post Your Assertive Discipline Plans for All to See. As soon as you have finished discussing your Discipline Plan with your child, post a copy of the plan in a prominent location, such as on the

---

*It is not appropriate when "laying down the law" to discuss positive rewards for good behavior. Discuss it at a later time when your children's behavior is under control.

refrigerator. This act will add additional impact to your verbal statements. In addition, the posted copy of the plan will serve as a reminder to your children that you do mean business and a reminder to you that you need to consistently follow through. On each sheet of paper you should write the child's name, the behaviors you have demanded that he or she follow, and what will happen if the child does not comply.

Brian will do his chores and homework right after school.

If he chooses not to, he will be grounded with no TV.

If you are using a Discipline Hierarchy, you can list the hierarchy of consequences. For example:

Deborah will follow directions immediately.

If she chooses not to:

The first time: Her name will be written on the chalkboard as a "warning."

The second time: She will receive a check and will be sent to the guest room for ten minutes.

The third time: Two checks and she will be sent to the guest room for twenty minutes and cannot watch TV for the remainder of the day.

The fourth time: Three checks and she will be sent to the guest room for thirty minutes and will go to bed early.

The chalkboard or the piece of paper you use for record-keeping should be placed right next to the Assertive Discipline Plan. One last point on this topic: If your children are too young to read, you may want to make stick-figure drawings to explain your rules and consequences.

WATCH OUT FOR THE "0-0-2-4-5-5-5" SYNDROME.

After you have laid down the law and begun carrying out the Discipline Plan you and your spouse have developed, you may run into the same problem that other parents face. That is, your children's behavior improves for a few days, but gradually the old problems reappear and soon enough the children are misbehaving as badly as ever.

Parents who reach this point with their children are so discouraged they often throw up their hands and say, "That does it. Nothing works with my children. It doesn't matter what I do. I give up."

The key reason that these parents have been unsuccessful in changing their children's behavior is that they have developed an inconsistent pattern of setting limits—a pattern we have labeled a "0-0-2-4-5-5-5" syndrome. Here is an example to illustrate what we mean.

Jack and Margaret were having problems dealing with their eight- and ten-year-olds' continual arguing and fighting. It seemed the two boys were at each other's throats whenever they were alone together. The problem was at its worst after dinner when the boys could not go outside and play. It got to the point where the parents had tried everything from yelling and screaming to taking away TV privileges and grounding.

One night when the boys were particularly disruptive, they had six arguments. Jack and Margaret sat down with them and laid down the law. "We have had it. There will be no more arguments or fights. If you choose to argue and fight after dinner, you will be sent to bed immediately. There will be no TV, no snack. This rule is in effect from now on!" Ten minutes later the boys were at it again. The parents, as they had said they would, sent them immediately to bed.

The first two nights after the parents cracked down, the boys were fine. There were no arguments. Jack and Margaret breathed a collective sigh of relief.

The third night the boys had two arguments. The parents responded with their usual yelling, "Cut it out," adding, "Don't make us send you to bed early." They thought about sending the boys to bed early as they had said they would, but agreed, "The boys were so much better than before, why bother?"

The fourth night the boys had four arguments. The parents again yelled and threatened to put them to bed early. They did not follow through again because they thought the boys were still not as "bad" as they had been.

From the fifth night on, the boys averaged five arguments per night. Both parents threw up their hands and said, "Nothing works with those boys. We sent them to bed early; they shaped up for a few days, and now they are at it again, as bad as ever."

Jack and Margaret typify the inconsistent 0-0-2-4-5-5-5 syndrome when dealing with chronic behavior problems. Namely, they would discipline their children and have a few days with no problem (0-0). Then when the problems gradually returned (2-4-5-5-5), the parents backed off and did not follow through as they had promised.

Parents such as Jack and Margaret who fall into the 0-0-2-4-5-5-5 syndrome do not realize the following:

Their disciplinary consequences *do* work. The boys *did* stop arguing for two days.

There is no quick fix when it comes to teaching children to change their chronic behavior. On the third day when the boys began to argue again, the parents should have sent them to their room as they said they would.

Consistency is the key to effective discipline. Nothing will work unless you, the parent, are prepared to back up your words with actions when your children's behavior requires you to do so.

Once again, the message you send by being consistent is this: I love you too much to allow you to misbehave without my responding. Avoid the 0-0-2-4-5-5-5 syndrome. Set limits every time your children choose to misbehave.

PULLING IT ALL TOGETHER

What we are saying in Step Three is that when all else fails you need to systematically plan how you will deal with your children's behavior. Once you have your plan, sit down with your children in a family session and lay down the law. Finally, and most importantly, you need to consistently follow through:

Child (angrily): I don't have to do what you say!

Parent (calmly putting a check on the discipline chart on the refrigerator): I told you that you can't talk back. That's the second time you did it today. You need to stay in your room for one hour this time.

Child (angrily): But I was just in my room. You just don't like me.

Parent (calmly): Kevin, it is your choice. We told you at the family meeting last night that we cannot tolerate your talking back. So, please go to your room.

For the rest of the day he is on his best behavior.

Parent: Kevin, I really like how cooperative you are. You have earned another star. When you get five more you will be allowed to rent a video movie.

Remember to create a balance. Set firm limits, then balance them with positive support.

POINTS TO REMEMBER:
LAY DOWN THE LAW

- When speaking assertively and backing up your words with actions is not enough, you and your spouse need to develop a systematic Assertive Discipline Plan.

- A systematic Assertive Discipline Plan is a written plan that includes:

  - The behaviors you want your children to change
  - The consequences you will utilize when your children misbehave
  - How you will monitor your children's behavior
  - How you will support your children's appropriate behavior

- Parent-saver techniques can be included in your systematic Assertive Discipline Plan.

  - A Discipline Hierarchy is useful for children who misbehave many times a day.
  - Positive Contracts are written agreements between you and your children. The child promises to behave; you promise to reward him or her.
  - Marble Mania helps motivate children to behave, especially in a family of two or more children.

- Your systematic Assertive Discipline Plan should be presented to your children in a lay-down-the-law meeting.

- Finally, be consistent. Avoid the 0-0-2-4-5-5-5 syndrome.

A FINAL THOUGHT

We want to conclude this section with a poem. It was given to us by a parent at one of our workshops and we have been unable to trace the author. We feel this poem best sums up what we are saying in the Assertive Discipline program.

Some day when my children are old enough to understand the logic that motivates a parent I will tell them:

I loved you enough to ask you where you were going, with whom, and what time you would be home.

I loved you enough to be silent and let you discover that your new best friend was a creep.

I loved you enough to stand over you for two hours while you cleaned your room. A job that would have taken me 15 minutes.

I loved you enough to let you assume the responsibility for your actions even when the penalties were so harsh they almost broke my heart

But most of all, I loved you enough to say "no" when I knew you would hate me for it.

Those were the most difficult battles of them all. I'm glad I won them because in the end you won something too.

—Anonymous

Stop!

You have just completed reading the three-step Assertive Discipline program for parents. You are now ready to put the ideas and techniques into action. If at any time you need help in determining positive or negative consequences, refer to the suggestions in Appendix 1.

The next section addresses special concerns that may or may not be applicable to you. The chapters include:

● Asking Your Spouse for Help with Discipline Problems.
● What to Do if Your Children Don't Behave in School.
● Commonly-Asked Questions.

Chapter 6   ASKING YOUR SPOUSE FOR HELP WITH DISCIPLINE PROBLEMS

Good discipline and teamwork are synonymous—you cannot have one without the other. In many households, though, one parent ends up with the weight of discipline on his or her shoulders. If this is the case in your family, there are ways to change it. In this chapter we will focus on how you can get the help you need to be a good disciplinarian.

At one of our recent Assertive Discipline Workshops, the following interchange occurred. An extremely upset and frustrated mother blurted out, "I feel I am the only one at home who deals with the kids. I swear my husband is oblivious to the way those kids carry on. There are times they just act awful. When I discipline the children, he simply will not support me. He just says, 'Kids will be kids.' I can't take it." A husband chimed in, "My wife is the same way. She always wants to be nice to the children, never wants to upset them. I always have to be the bad guy, and the children complain I'm picking on them. I feel just like you. I don't know what to do!" Both these parents are feeling the burden of trying to discipline their children single-handedly. They both need to assert themselves and get the help they deserve from their spouses.

The first step for those parents—or any parent in a similar situation—to get help is to recognize the fact that you, the parent, have the right to ask for it. When there are two parents in the house, those two parents must work together when dealing with the children. We know you are aware that your children test repeatedly to see if both you and your spouse mean what you say and say what you mean. If your children pick up from one of you that they have to follow your directions, yet sense that the other parent does not really care, the children will continue to misbehave. In two-parent homes, one parent can rarely get the children to behave without the active support of his or her spouse.

Let's look at how you can assert yourself with your spouse in order to get more support in dealing with the discipline problems of your children. Initially you will need to discriminate between the effective and ineffective responses you can make to him or her. To help you accomplish this, we again need to turn to the concept of assertive, nonassertive and hostile responses.

When you respond in an assertive manner to your spouse, you will clearly and firmly communicate your wants and needs. From our work with families we have determined that a clear, direct "I" message is usually the most appropriate and effective statement you can make. "I want you to please help me with the children." "I need your help in disciplining our children." Such a direct assertive response will maximize the possibility of your getting what you need in your interaction with your spouse.

TIP   Avoid strong statements, like "you will help me with the children or else." Statements like this will only alienate your spouse.

The effective assertive response again needs to be compared to the ineffective nonassertive and hostile responses you can make to your spouse. When you respond in a nonassertive manner, you do not clearly or firmly state your wants or needs: "Why don't you try to do something with the kids?" This kind of indirect response does not communicate what you truly want your spouse to do. When you respond in a hostile manner, you respond in a way that criticizes or possibly degrades your spouse: "It's just disgusting how you let the kids act up and run all over you!" Such a response, in all probability, will provoke your spouse and will not help the two of you to work together.

To further help you discriminate between these assertive, nonassertive and hostile responses, here is an example of what we mean:

Joan was having problems trying to handle her teenage son, David. Her husband, Gil, worked long hours and when he came home he did not want to be bothered with all her complaints regarding their son. Joan was near the end of her rope and wanted more help in disciplining David.

Joan initially approached her husband in a nonassertive manner, feeling she was a failure due to her inability to handle their son. All she ever said to her husband were indirect comments such as, "I'm having some problems again with David." Her husband would respond in his typically brusque manner, "Look, you're home with him. You do whatever you want. I'm sure it will be fine." Unfortunately, Joan would not pursue the conversation any further.

The problems with her son grew and so did her frustration and anger. Her anger eventually erupted, and one day she lashed out at her husband in a hostile manner. "I'm sick and tired of you never doing anything about our son's behavior. Why don't you do something to the kid!" Those comments only made her husband defensive and provoked an argument.

After attending one of our workshops, Joan realized she must have help with her son and that there was nothing wrong with asking for it. She sat down with her husband and told him in a clear, assertive manner, "I must have some help with David's behavior. I cannot handle him without more support from you!" Those comments were the beginning of a productive conversation about how her husband could help her deal with their son's behavior.

HOW TO GET HELP FROM YOUR SPOUSE

In order to help you respond in an assertive manner to your spouse, we have developed the following guidelines for you to follow.

Plan How You Will Present Your Concerns to Your Spouse. When you are in conflict with your spouse regarding his or her role in the discipline of your children, we have found that it is extremely useful to plan what you will say before you discuss the problem with him or her. Here is how we suggest you prepare before you talk with your spouse.

● **Decide upon goals for the discussion.** What do you want from your spouse? In most instances you will want his or her cooperation and support in dealing with the discipline problems of your children.

I need more cooperation from you, Dear, in dealing with the children.

- **What are your specific objectives?** How do you specifically want your spouse to reach the aforementioned goals? In what ways do you want him or her to help out or change?

  I want you to help me set up a Discipline Plan for the children.

  I want you to discipline the children when they act up in front of you.

- **What is the rationale for the discussion?** In the majority of discussions with your spouse, your reason for such talks will be as follows:

  It is in our children's best interests that they know we are a team and that we will both deal with them when they do or do not behave.

- **State the consequences you feel will occur** if your spouse does not offer the support you need. Be straightforward! Don't beat around the bush. Let your spouse know what you feel will occur if he or she does not give you the support you need with the children.

  Unless you support me with the children, I feel I simply will not be able to get them to behave, and this house will become even more chaotic!

  Unless you follow through on the Assertive Discipline Plan, I feel we will continue to have all of this tension in the house.

  Unless you back me up in getting our child to behave, I think he will never learn to act appropriately.

Use the worksheet on page 122 of Appendix 2 to help you plan your communication with your spouse.

> TIP   Set aside a specific time when you and your spouse can sit down undisturbed and discuss your concerns at length.

When Appropriate, Utilize Assertive Communication Skills. Some spouses have great difficulty discussing the discipline of their children. They may become hostile, evasive, defensive, or accusatory. If this is the case with your spouse, it would be helpful to use the communication skill we mentioned to you earlier—the broken record.

Broken Record. This technique is, again, designed to help you make your point and stick to it. To utilize this technique, you need to determine what you want from your interaction with your spouse. This should take the form of a statement: ''I need your cooperation in regard to our children's behavior,'' etc. In your interaction with your spouse, the broken record will be evidenced by the repeated expression of your message, thereby disregarding the ''sidetracking'' responses of your spouse.

Wife: I need your cooperation to make sure the children do their chores and homework on the nights that I work late. [Statement of want]

Husband: Look, I know I have to be more involved with the kids, but I'm beat when I get home. [Sidetracking]

Wife: I understand, Dear, but you still need to make sure that they do their chores and their homework. [Broken record]

Husband: You sure are persistent.

Wife: You're right. The kids need to know it is just as important to you as it is to me that they do their chores and homework.

Husband: I see your point. I will make sure they get everything done.

TIP   Point out to your spouse the benefits to the entire family if the child is better behaved.

Involve Your Spouse in Planning the Discipline Effort with Your Children. The more you involve a reluctant spouse in determining your children's Assertive Discipline Plan, the higher probability you will have of getting his or her support. Do not sit down with your spouse and flatly state, "Here is what the kids have to do differently and here is how to both discipline and reward the children."

To help you further understand the point we have just made about getting support from a reluctant spouse, here is an example of a parent utilizing these ideas.

Ethel and Roger both worked at careers. Many nights they did not get home until just before dinner. There were constant problems with the children, especially at this time, due to the children's "forgetting" to set the table, help fix dinner, and general disobedience. Roger did not like conflict, and whenever possible he would let Ethel handle the children. Ethel reached the point where she needed more support in handling the children, so she sat down with Roger and they had the following conversation.

Ethel: I am really fed up with the children. I feel I'm at them all the time and it does no good. Roger, I need your help in getting the children to behave. [Goal]

Roger: What's the problem now, Ethel?

Ethel: The kids don't help us get ready for dinner. They constantly argue with me and don't listen to a word I say.

Roger: You know, I think you just get too upset with those kids. Don't pay any attention to them.

Ethel: I understand your feelings, Roger, but I still need your help in getting the kids to behave. [Broken record]

Roger: Well, what do you want me to do?

Ethel: I need your help in setting up an Assertive Discipline Plan to. . . .

Roger: What in the world is an Assertive Discipline Plan?

Ethel: In this book I just read, it states that it is helpful to set up rules for the kids to follow as well as consequences for behaving and misbehaving. I want you to help me set up the rules and the things we will do when they are good and when they are bad.

Roger: You usually discipline the kids. Why don't you just do it yourself?

Ethel: The kids must know we are working together, Roger, to make sure they behave. We cannot allow them to act as they do. We can't let them grow up acting like this. [Rationale]

Roger: Well, I think this Discipline Plan is going a little too far.

Ethel: I understand, Roger, but I need your support to get the kids to behave. I feel the plan is the best way to go. [Broken record]

Roger: You sure are serious about this, Dear, aren't you?

Ethel: You bet I am. The kids don't feel you are behind me, and that makes it impossible for me around here. Unless you give me more support, I've had it. You try handling the kids by yourself. Unless something is done, the stress will get to me! [Consequence]

Roger: I didn't realize it was so bad. Tell me what we need to start this Discipline Plan. I'll help you with it, and I'll let the kids know they must shape up!

TIP   Support a spouse who agrees to help. All people need positive reinforcement.

Please note: If your spouse is not very cooperative in relation to disciplining the children, it may prove helpful to ask him or her to read this book. Your spouse may thus gain a better understanding of how you arrived at your ideas and, in addition, may be more willing to accept the ideas from experts in child behavior rather than from his or her spouse.

One last point: If your spouse has become an ex-spouse, it may be much more difficult to get his or her support in dealing with the children. It will be even more important to follow the ideas we have just presented in this chapter.

TIP   You have a right to support from an ex-spouse, too.

In this chapter we have discussed how to ask your spouse for help. Here are the points we want you to remember: You have a right to ask your spouse for help in dealing with your children's misbehavior. In order to maximize the effectiveness of your communication with your spouse you should respond in an assertive manner. Finally, you should plan what you are going to say to your spouse before you meet.

POINTS TO REMEMBER:
ASKING FOR HELP WITH DISCIPLINE PROBLEMS

- If your spouse will not help you with your children's behavior, recognize that you have a right to receive help.

- Be assertive. Clearly and firmly let your spouse know what you need.

- Avoid ineffective nonassertive or hostile responses to your spouse.

- Plan how you will discuss your concerns with your spouse:

  Decide your goal: I need your cooperation with the children.
  Decide your objectives: I need you to help me with our son's fighting.
  Decide your rationale: It is in our child's best interest that we work together as a team.

- When necessary use assertive communication skills such as the broken record. Involve your spouse in the planning of your discipline efforts.

Chapter 7   BUT WHAT IF THEY DON'T BEHAVE IN SCHOOL?

We are well aware that many of your children have had problems behaving at school as well as at home. In this chapter we will spell out in detail how you can work with your children's teachers and principal in order to prevent problems from developing and to eliminate them if they occur. First, some background information pertaining to the behavior problems in today's schools is necessary.

We want to begin by sharing with you some important, down-to-earth facts to be aware of when working with your children's teachers.

Teachers don't like to call parents and tell them they are having a problem with their children. Teachers have been told that they should be able to handle all behavior problems on their own with no help from parents. This is nonsense; yet many teachers and principals still hold to this misguided belief. As a result, teachers usually put off calling you until the problem with your children has become serious. In addition, they will tend to downplay the problem they are having in order not to look bad or upset you. For example, teachers typically say, "We are having a small problem with your child's attitude," etc. Don't be misled. If a teacher or principal contacts you, there is a problem that needs to be dealt with, and your help is definitely required.

Because teachers are reluctant to admit they can't handle their students, it is not uncommon for a child to have had problems for several years and his or her teachers not to have contacted the parents. Thus, when out of the blue your child's teacher calls and explains the problem he or she is having with your child, you may feel (especially after listening to your child) that the teacher is picking on your child or that there is a personality conflict between them. The reality is that in all probability the teacher is a skilled professional who is concerned enough about your child to work with you to help the child.

> TIP   Make it a point to respond in writing or on the phone to all correspondence from your child's teacher. Let the teacher know you are interested in taking an active part in your child's education.

There are several reasons why your children's teachers must have your cooperation in helping your children to shape up. First, your children's teachers just do not have the "clout" our teachers did. When our teachers told us to "do it," we responded, "How quickly?" Many of today's students may respond with a blasé "I don't feel like doing it" or a flat-out "No!" Your children must know you are one hundred percent behind their teachers and that you will go to any means necessary to support them. Second, you obviously know your children better than their teachers know them. You know best what your children would dislike happening to them if they act up and, on the other hand, what could be used as motivation to reward them if they do behave.

HOW TO WORK SUCCESSFULLY WITH YOUR CHILD'S SCHOOL

Now, let us turn our attention to the specific details of how to work successfully with your children's teacher or principal.

Determine the Specific Problems Your Child Is Having at School. When your child's teacher, principal, or counselor contacts you regarding a problem with the child at school, determine the exact nature of the problem. Do not settle for "He's been bad" or "She has to change her attitude." Ask questions: What does my child do wrong? When does he or she do it? How often does it occur? When does it occur? Ask for any documentation of the problem: for example, incomplete work, the school's discipline records. Through your questioning, you will want to achieve a clear picture of the nature and severity of your child's problems.

It will be useful to determine also what the teacher or principal has done in the past in response to your child's misbehavior. What type of discipline have they utilized? What type of positive support have they utilized? What approaches have worked? What approaches have not worked? This information will help serve as a baseline upon which to build future responses to your child's behavior at school. To further illustrate how to work with your child's school we will follow the example of a concerned parent we worked with.

Mrs. Lewis received a call from her son Brian's sixth-grade teacher, Ms. Kerry, regarding his constant problems at school. In the course of the conversation, Brian's mother came to understand that, rather than do his work in class, he would act silly and disrupt the children around him. Ms. Kerry reported that she had tried taking away his recess and free-time privileges when he acted up and praising him when he behaved, but this simply was not working.

Determine a School-Home Assertive Discipline Plan for Your Child. Team work between home and school is necessary if you want your child to improve his or her behavior. You and your child's teacher—and possibly vice-principal, principal, or counselor—will want to set up a School-Home Assertive Discipline Plan for guidelines on how you will all respond to your child's behavior. The School-Home Assertive Discipline Plan is similar to an Assertive Discipline Plan. It will (1) specify the behavior you want your child to follow at school and (2) detail how the teacher and, if necessary, the principal will respond when your child does, or does not, behave. The plan will also (3) include your responses when you receive feedback about your child's school behavior. In other words, the School-Home Assertive Discipline Plan is designed so that, depending upon how your child behaves, he or she will be disciplined or rewarded both at school and at home.

Whenever possible, we recommend that you go to school and meet with your child's teacher and principal. Face-to-face contact is advantageous when you are dealing with such serious problems as those related to your child's misbehavior at school.

In your discussions with your child's teacher and principal, you will need to determine what they specifically expect from your child and what negative and positive consequences they will provide your child for his or her behavior. In most instances, especially if the teacher is using Assertive Discipline, he or she will already have this information available and may have previously shared it with you.

If your child's teacher does not have a plan, we would strongly recommend that you suggest the need to set one up with your child. (See worksheet on page 123 of Appendix 2.)

Your child's misbehavior may occur outside of the classroom—in the halls, on the playing field, or in the cafeteria—and the school principal or vice-principal may be the one responsible for dealing with your child. If this is the case, ascertain the plan of action the principal or vice-principal has decided to utilize with your child.

Once you understand how the school will deal with your child, determine what assistance you can give. In most instances, it will be beneficial if you back up the school by rewarding or disciplining the child at home, depending upon the "good" or "bad" report that you receive from the school.

Finally, your efforts with the school must be based upon solid, day-by-day monitoring of your child's behavior by telephone or, more commonly, by note. Each day the teacher or principal will need to send you a note indicating how your child behaved and how you should follow through at home. Conversely, each morning you will need to send the teacher a note indicating your efforts at home. Let's go back to our example of Mrs. Lewis and her son Brian.

Brian's mother went to school and met with Ms. Kerry. They agreed that it was in Brian's best interest that they set up a School-Home Assertive Discipline Plan to help him.

Ms. Kerry determined the following rules Brian must follow in class: Do what I tell you to do. Do your work. Do not talk or disrupt the children sitting next to you.

She decided that if Brian broke a rule, she would utilize these consequences:

The first time he broke a rule: His name would be put on the board.
The second time he broke a rule: He would spend twenty minutes sitting alone in the back of the class.
The third time he broke a rule: He would spend forty minutes sitting alone in the back of the class.
The fourth time he broke a rule: He would be sent to the principal's office to do his work.

Ms. Kerry decided that when Brian did behave he would earn a star, and when he earned ten stars he would receive a Positive Citizen Award, which was the big reward that all the children in class wanted.

The mother and the teacher further agreed that Mrs. Lewis should follow through at home. Every day Ms. Kerry would send a note home with Brian indicating how he had behaved that day in class. If he had not completed his work, the assignment would accompany the note, and his mother would see that he finished it at home. If the note indicated that Brian had misbehaved, his mother would not allow him to watch TV that night. If the note indicated that he had behaved, she would give him a point, and when he had earned five points, she would take him to buy a fish for his aquarium.

TIP   Post positive notes from your child's teacher on the refrigerator or on a bulletin board.

Sit Down with Your Child and Share the School-Home Assertive Discipline Plan. Once you and the school staff have determined your plan of action, we strongly recommend that you, the teacher, and any other school personnel involved, sit down face-to-face with your child and, as a group, "lay down the law." Your child must know that he or she has to behave at school and that both home and school are working together to help motivate the child to shape up.

The child should be presented with the specifics of the School-Home Assertive Discipline Plan. The child must know the behaviors he or she must engage in; what the school staff will do if the child does, or does not, behave; and how you will follow through at home.

When Brian's mother and teacher had completed their plan, they sat down with Brian and clearly asserted their demands.

Ms. Kerry: Brian, you will do your work in my class—without disrupting!

Mrs. Lewis: Brian, I will not tolerate your behavior at school. You will do whatever your teacher tells you.

Brian: You don't understand. It's not my fault. . . .

Mrs. Lewis (interrupting): That's not the point. You will do what Ms. Kerry says!

They then proceeded to tell Brian what they both would do if he did, or did not, behave in class. His mother concluded the conversation by stating:
Brian, you are very fortunate to have a teacher like Ms. Kerry who cares so much about you. I will not see you fail at school. We are going to work together to help you, and you will improve your behavior.

Make Sure You and the School Follow Through on the Plan. Keep on top of the implementation of your School-Home Assertive

Discipline Plan. Follow through each night at home, rewarding or disciplining your child in accordance with the feedback you receive from school. Monitor the school's efforts. Is the teacher sending you home a note every day? Does the note indicate what you are to do? Is the teacher disciplining your child in class if he or she misbehaves? Is the teacher reinforcing your child in class if he or she behaves? Is the principal or vice-principal following through if necessary?

TIP   **Either call the principal or send a note explaining what a fine job your child's teacher has done.**

If, on the other hand, your child's teacher is not following through and working with you as planned, be sure to call him or her and determine why. If you are not satisfied with the response, it may be appropriate to ask the teacher to arrange a meeting with you and the principal to discuss the matter further.

It is important to be aware that the vast majority of teachers are excellent professionals. There are, though, a small percentage of teachers who, for various reasons—frustration, "burn-out," incompetence—do not put forth the effort necessary to deal effectively with children and parents. If this is the case, it is in your best interest and your child's best interest that, after talking with the teacher, you arrange a meeting with the principal to resolve the matter. Back to our example of Mrs. Lewis and Brian.

Each day in class, Ms. Kelly closely monitored Brian's behavior. Misbehavior resulted in his being sent to do his work alone in the back of the class, while appropriate behavior was greeted with, "Good work, Brian. Here's another star." Each afternoon, his mother read the note from the teacher and responded accordingly at home.

Dear Mrs. Lewis:

Today Brian's behavior was unacceptable. He disrupted twice in class and did not finish his math. It would be helpful if you made sure he finishes his math and, as we discussed, take away TV privileges because of his disruptions in class.

Sincerely, Ms. Kerry

Within one week Brian had begun to improve his behavior. He had earned two Positive Citizen Awards and one tropical fish.

Within two weeks his mother and his teacher decided to cut the notes down from daily to weekly because Brian had turned his behavior around and was doing his work without any problems.

When your child's behavior has improved, you will want to phase out the notes from daily to weekly and then, when appropriate, stop them. We suggest, though, that you still periodically call your child's teacher or principal to make sure your child is behaving in an appropriate manner.

We have one last point for this chapter. The key to your children's behavior at school is your involvement and support of the teachers' efforts with them. Too many of today's parents have the attitude that "my children are the school's responsibility from 9:00 to 3:00." Your children must know that you, in no uncertain terms, will not tolerate their misbehavior at school. Your children must know that you consider their teacher as the boss in the classroom and they are to do whatever he or she says. In conclusion, your children must know you expect them to behave at school—no ifs, ands, or buts!

In this chapter we have discussed how to deal with your children's misbehavior at school. Your children's teachers and principal must have your help in dealing with your children's behavior at school. You should set up a School-Home Assertive Discipline Plan to help structure your efforts with your children. Finally, always remember that your children must know you will not tolerate their misbehavior at school.

POINTS TO REMEMBER:
WHEN YOUR CHILDREN HAVE BEHAVIOR PROBLEMS AT
SCHOOL

You must support the school's efforts with your children's behavior. When the school contacts you, determine the specific problems your children are having.

Set up a School-Home Assertive Discipline Plan.

Determine the behaviors to be worked on.

Determine how the teacher and the principal will handle the problem at school.

Determine how you need to support the school at home.

You, the teacher, and the principal should sit down with the children and discuss the School-Home Assertive Discipline Plan.

Be sure to follow through and make sure the school consistently deals with your children's behavior problems.

Chapter 8   QUESTIONS AND ANSWERS

Here are the most commonly asked questions parents have regarding their use of Assertive Discipline.

GENERAL PHILOSOPHY

Question: I feel that by demanding my children just ''stop'' their problem behavior, I will never deal with the feelings that lie behind their actions. How do you respond to this?

Response: It is vital, even critical, for parents to deal with their children's feelings. We are not suggesting you don't. However, there comes a time when your children's misbehavior, if allowed to continue, will become disruptive to you, your household, and themselves. At that time you must be able to be firm and get them to stop this inappropriate behavior. Once things are under control, it is your responsibility as a loving parent to sit down with your children and help them explore, express, and deal with the feelings that lie behind, and that may cause, their problem behavior.

Question: Don't you feel you must understand why your children are misbehaving before you can realistically help them change their behavior?

Response: Ideally, you would want to know why your children are misbehaving before you attempted to help them change their behavior. There is one major problem in this concept. With most children we can do no more than speculate as to why they are misbehaving. One school of thought maintains that the cause of children's misbehavior may be a result of their early feeding habits, toilet training, or relations with their mother and father. Even if you knew one of these past experiences was the cause, what good would it do you? Rather than putting extensive energy into determining why your children are misbehaving, place that same energy into formulating a plan of action for how you will deal with it. You will benefit from this approach and so will your children.

Question: I've been what you would label a "nonassertive" parent. Won't it have a detrimental effect on my children if all of a sudden I make a dramatic change?

Response: First off, don't run around your house and start wildly sending your children to their rooms. You will need to sit down with your children and explain to them that their past misbehavior has been unacceptable and what you are going to be doing about it. Next, please do not worry about your children. I guarantee you, they are much more adaptable than you are. The main impact that your being more assertive will have on your children is that they will improve their behavior, stop their "hassling," and have a better relationship with you. We have never heard of children suffering psychological trauma from their parents' becoming more effective in how they deal with them.

Question: I am afraid that if I crack down hard on my twelve-year-old for minor problems, such as staying out too late or not listening to us, I will not have any disciplinary methods left if she acts bad. What do you have to say about this?

Response: Many parents share your feelings. But experience shows us very clearly that, unless you've set limits on your child's minor problems, by the time he or she engages in major problems (drugs, for example) you may have lost so much control that there will be no means left for you to use to influence the child's behavior.

Question: My son is in therapy, and his counselor feels he is not emotionally ready for me to confront him. What should I do?

Response: If your child is currently seeing a professional counselor, we firmly believe you should listen to him or her. Under no circumstances alter how you are dealing with your child unless you discuss it thoroughly with your child's counselor. This book is not a replacement for professional counseling for your child.

Question: I feel my child's problems are directly related to the fact that I am a working mother. What do you have to say about this?

Response: We are very tired of hearing that because a mother works, the children will have problems. There is no direct relationship between the two conditions. Just because you work does not mean you are incapable of dealing with your child's behavior.

SINGLE OR DIVORCED PARENTS

Question: I'm a single parent. How do I find the time or energy to be as consistent as you say is necessary?

Response: We are well aware that being a single parent makes the job of disciplining your children much more difficult. But you still can be consistent; you still can be effective. Stop believing that just because you are a single parent you cannot get your children to behave. You can, and if you follow the guidelines presented in this book, you will be able to.

Question: I am divorced and my ex-husband constantly tells our children that I am too hard on them and that they really don't need to listen to me. What do you suggest?

Response: Obviously, you need to tell your ex-husband that what he is saying to the children is not in their best interests. If you cannot get him to stop making statements like that to your children, it will be necessary for you to sit down with your children and tell them very clearly that no matter what their father says, when they are with you, you are the boss and they are going to have to follow your rules.

Question: I'm a single parent who works. How can I find the time to reinforce my children's good behavior as needed?

Response: We admit it is more difficult to give your children positive attention being a single parent who works, but it still can be done. You will need to set aside time each day when you can focus on the positive aspects of your children's behavior. The effort will be well worth it.

Question: My wife and I have been divorced for three years and, to say the least, she does not believe in disciplining the children. When they come to spend the weekend with me, they act like wild animals. I don't like being the bad guy and laying down the law. Do you have any other suggestions?

Response: Please do not feel you are the "bad guy" when you expect your children to act appropriately. In the long run your children will come to appreciate the fact that you care enough about them to expect them to behave in an appropriate manner when they are with you on the weekend.

Question: I'm divorced and whenever I discipline my children they get upset and demand to go live with their father. What do you suggest?

Response: This is not an uncommon problem. You are going to have to let your children know that when they are with you they will have to behave in a manner that you feel is in their best interest. Many children use threats of wanting to go to the other parent as a means to manipulate the disciplining parent into giving in. If this is the case with you, we recommend it's in your best interest and their best interest that you stand your ground.

POSITIVE SUPPORT

Question: We really believe in praising our children for everything they do right. But lately, the more we praise them, the more they act up. What are we doing wrong?

Response: Two things. First, your children probably are being over-praised by you. If you go around your house saying, "I like . . ." everything your children do, after a while praise will lose all its meaning for your children. Second, how about setting some limits when your children misbehave? Don't forget, you must balance your positive responses with appropriate limits.

Question: My parents were not big on praising us when we were good and I grew up okay. Why do I really need to be different with my kids?

Response: Experience has taught us that the more positive you are with your children, the easier it will be to get them to behave. Your parents may not have needed to utilize reinforcement with you and your brothers and sisters, but times are different. If you choose not to utilize reinforcement, be aware that you are choosing to make it more difficult to get your children to behave.

Question: When we ask our children what they would like to earn by their good behavior, all they come up with are toys that are too expensive for us to buy. What do you suggest?

Response: You need to let your children know you cannot afford such expensive rewards and that you are willing to consider less costly alternatives. You should go through the reinforcement worksheet questions in the Appendix 3 and select alternatives your children would want. Don't be intimidated into providing your children with rewards you are not comfortable utilizing.

SETTING LIMITS

Question: My children say I am mean and they become upset when I respond to them in what you describe as an assertive manner. If what I am doing is right, why do they get so upset?

Response: Your children are testing your limits. Children always want to know if you truly mean business. In the past they may have learned that if they raised a big fuss and caused you enough hassles, you would back down. It is in your best interest, as well as your children's, to resist their attempts to manipulate you. Stand up for your wants and needs and do what you feel is best.

Question: Whenever I use the "broken record" on my son, he gets angry and yells at me to stop repeating myself. What should I do?

Response: Tell your son that if he does not like your using the "broken record" and repeating yourself, he should listen to you the first time you tell him something.

Question: You state that you must follow through with a disciplinary consequence every time a child breaks one of your rules. Yesterday my child broke one of my rules and I forgot to follow through. What do you suggest?

Response: Just because you did not follow through once does not mean all is lost. Being human, we all respond inconsistently at times to our children's behavior. We recommend that you let your child know that you forgot to follow through but that you will not forget in the future.

Question: I am afraid that if I respond as consistently as you say, I would do nothing but discipline my children all day long. Is this so?

Response: You are not alone in your fear. Most parents feel as you do. To be honest, your fear and the fears of other parents are groundless. Your children may act up for a while, but when you set firm limits, they will soon recognize that you mean business and that there is nothing in it for them to continue misbehaving.

Question: Why is it that you repeatedly use grounding, sending a child to his or her room, and taking away a privilege as disciplinary consequences?

Response: Sending a child to his or her room, grounding and taking away privileges are suggested frequently because, from our experience in working with parents, we have determined that these are consequences parents often use that work. We have found, however, that the key to dealing with your children's misbehavior is not what consequences you use but how you use them. Any consequence, when used consistently, will prove highly effective in motivating the vast majority of children to improve their behavior.

Question: My twelve-year-old threatens to run away if I set up an Assertive Discipline Plan. How would you handle that?

Response: We have a question for you. Who runs your house, you or your twelve-year-old? If you allow the threats of your children to deter you as a parent from dealing responsibly with your family, you are in trouble. You must let your child know that you, not she, decide what will happen in the household and that if she runs away, she will be dealt with firmly.

Question: We often have problems with our children's behavior when we go out to eat at a restaurant. Do you have any suggestions?

Response: Here is an idea one father we worked with presented that proved highly effective. His children were continuously disruptive whenever they went out to eat. It was rare that a meal at a restaurant wasn't punctuated with yelling and screaming by all the children. The father had tried everything he could think of, to no avail. Finally he came up with the following plan. He told the children, "If any one of you disrupts when we go out to the restaurant tonight, we will all come home immediately and whoever disrupted will go right to bed." Soon after they arrived at the restaurant his youngest son began to be disruptive. The father cancelled the order with the waitress, put all the kids in the car, and drove home. His son was escorted immediately to bed. Not only was his son unhappy about going to bed early, he had to bear the brunt of brothers and sisters being unhappy that they were deprived of a meal at their favorite restaurant. The father had to demonstrate his concern by using such a strong consequence only once.

Question: My teenager continually lies to me about where she is. I have tried everything. Do you have any ideas about what I can do?

Response: We worked with a father who had the same problem with his daughter. Nothing he tried worked until he told his daughter he would allow her to go out—on one condition. Every hour or two she must call him and report where she was. Periodically, he would have her stay at the reported location and he would drive there to make sure she was where she had told him she was. The father did not like doing this. The daughter liked it even less. However, after a few weeks this method produced results, and the father was able to monitor her behavior effectively and ensure she was telling the truth. Please note: This is a strong approach to dealing with a teenager and should be used only when all else has failed.

Question: I think grounding my children at home punishes me more than them. Having them around the house is sometimes just too much for me to handle. What do you suggest?

Response: Any consequence that you use with your children, you must be comfortable with. If you are not comfortable grounding your children, do not use that as a consequence when your children misbehave. Come up with some other consequence (taking away a privilege, etc.) that you feel would best meet your needs.

Question: When my kids misbehave, I take away TV. The problem I have, though, is that the kids wander around the house and "bug" me, complaining that they have nothing to do. What do you suggest?

Response: If, when you take TV away from your children, they begin to bother you, we would recommend that you tell your children very clearly that unless they find something to do, you may have to put them in their rooms so that they will stop bothering you. Many children try to punish the parents for taking TV away by harassing them. Don't allow this.

Question: My children are often late for school because they are watching TV and do not get ready in time. I have thus set up a plan that they can not watch TV until they are dressed in the morning. The problem is, they still watch TV. What can I do?

Response: It will be necessary for you to monitor your children more closely in the morning to make sure they get dressed without watching TV. You may also want to consider unplugging the TV in the morning so the children cannot watch it.

Question: When I demand that my son do what I want he just smirks and walks away. What do you have to say about this situation?

Response: Our question to you is: What do you do when your son walks away? You are not going to be the boss with a child like this if you tolerate his walking away from you when you lay down the law. We worked with a mother who had a problem similar to yours, and later she reported the following incident. On one occasion when her son walked away from her she grabbed him firmly by the arm, looked him in the eye, and told him, "You will never do that again!" We asked her what she would have done if her son hadn't listened to her, and she told us, "I was prepared to pull out all the stops. I would have grounded him for as long as it took for that boy to realize he could never, ever talk to me that way again." Such sincere determination may be necessary for you to get your point across to your child.

Question: My daughter is constantly in trouble at home and at school. Whenever I do assert myself as you say and discipline her in a firm, consistent manner, she does improve her behavior. The problem is that she gets very upset with me and accuses me of being unfair and overly harsh. After a few days of listening to her I tend to back down, and the problems begin all over again. What do you suggest?

Response: Your daughter obviously has found a way to manipulate you when you lay down the law. Don't feel bad—you are not alone. Many parents react as you do. The message we want to send you is that even though your daughter may be unhappy with you, you are doing the right thing. There is nothing you can do that is more harmful to your child than to allow her to continue to misbehave without responding in a firm, consistent manner. Keep up the firm, consistent limits. Be sure to balance them with praise when your daughter improves her behavior. If you stick to your guns, we'll wager that after a few days your daughter will stop her complaining.

Question: My child often gets into trouble when he is at a neighbor's house, and I don't find out about it until several hours later. Is it still okay to discipline him when it is long after the behavior occurs?

Response: The key to providing the consequence is that you provide it immediately after you become aware of the behavior. Tell your child that "I just found out how you behaved at the neighbor's house" and then tell him or her what is going to occur.

SCHOOL BEHAVIOR PROBLEMS.

Question: My son says it's not fair that I discipline him at home for his misbehavior at school because he was disciplined by his teacher for the behavior. What do you have to say to this?

Response: Let your child know it would be even less fair for you not to discipline him at home for his misbehavior. Let him know that you and the school are working together as a team to make sure he behaves in a manner that is in his best interest at school.

Question: I set up a Behavior Contract with my child's teacher, but she has not followed through on the plan. She says she's too busy to send notes home every day about how my child misbehaves. What can I do?

Response: First, contact the teacher and let her know that you want to know each day how your child behaves at school. If that does not work, go to the principal and tell him or her that you need more support from the teacher in order to deal with your child's inappropriate behavior at school.

Question: My child always says the other kids in class act up so much that they cause him to get worked up and misbehave. What do you have to say to this?

Response: Inform your child that he is responsible for his own behavior. Let him know that no other child can make him act up in class. He, not the other children, is in control of his actions, and you will accept no excuses for his misbehavior at school.

Question: My child got a terrible report card because of his misbehavior. I had no idea there were any problems at school. What do you suggest?

Response: Demand a meeting with your child's teacher. Let the teacher know you are extremely unhappy that you had not been informed earlier about your child's problems. Establish a plan of action with that teacher to help your child improve his behavior at school. If you do not get satisfaction from the teacher, Immediately go to the principal and share your concerns. As a parent, you have the right to know how your child behaves at school, and there is no reason for a teacher not informing you!

Question: My child is always getting into trouble at school due to his fighting. He says the other kids provoke him. What do you suggest?

Response: Firmly let your child know that you will not tolerate his fighting at school for any reason. Talk to him about alternative behavior he can engage in other than fighting with the children when he is provoked.

Question: Isn't it really more effective just to allow the school to handle my children's problems that occur there?

Response: Absolutely not! Too many parents believe that the child's behavior at school is the school's responsibility to handle. As we stated before, your children must know that you and the school are both working together.

Question: My daughter was bad at school, and the teacher kept her afterwards. As a result, she missed the bus, and I had to come to get her. I was very put out about it. What can I do about this?

Response: If you do not like having to pick up your child at school, we recommend that you tell your child to listen to the teacher so that she will not have to be disciplined. If your child's behavior is such that she must be kept after school for disciplinary reasons, it should be a clear message to you to let your child know she had better improve her behavior at school.

Question: My son behaves fine at home, but he is a real problem at school. Could it be the school's fault?

Response: It is possible that the teacher is not handling your child correctly. It is more probable that your child simply does not behave at school. Just because your child, in your opinion, behaves at home, it does not necessarily follow that he behaves in other situations—including school. In all too many cases today, parents tend to blame schools for their child's problems. We recommend that you sit down with your child's teacher and principal, hear what they have to say, and take their comments very seriously.

Question: My teenager is a severe behavior problem at school. He is often tardy, and when he does get to class he is very disruptive. We have tried everything with him, including disciplining him at home and suspending him from school. Do you have any ideas?

Response: When you have tried everything else with a child who is such a problem at school, there is one approach you may want to attempt. With the approval of the school, you or your spouse may want to attend your child's classes and monitor his behavior for the entire day. A mother we worked with did this and reported the following. "My son was constantly in trouble at school. Both the school personnel and I got fed up, so I decided to spend an entire day with him at school. I made sure he got to class and I sat in the back of each class to make sure he behaved. My son hated this, to say the least.

He reported to me at the end of the day, 'I never want this to happen again.' I told him I felt the same way. Ever since that time he has behaved. I didn't like doing it, but it produced results when all else had failed.'' Using the same technique when all else has failed may get results for you as well.

Question: Our son is always in trouble at school. We have grounded him, taken away TV, and nothing works. All he cares about is Little League. I hate to take that away from him. How do you feel about this?

Response: What is more important to you—your child's behaving at school or his taking part in Little League? Your child may have to know that he will choose to miss Little League if he disrupts at school. Without that reality hanging over his head, he may not accept that you do mean business.

Appendix 1 **DISCIPLINARY AND POSITIVE CONSEQUENCES**

In this appendix we will list resource ideas which can serve as the consequences to be utilized when your children do, or do not, behave. All the consequences presented have been successfully utilized by parents. We want to emphasize a vital point: You must be comfortable using any consequence, positive or negative, that you choose. Please do not take any idea we present and use it unless you and your spouse both feel it is appropriate for your family.

We will begin with disciplinary consequences which you may find useful. The first consequences we present are those designed to be used with minor behavior problems. They will be followed by those designed to be used with serious behavior problems.

We define minor behavior problems as "annoying," run-of-the-mill misbehavior most children engage in from time to time. These problems can cover a wide range: "forgetting" to follow directions, "hassling" you when it is time to get ready for school or at bedtime, sibling rivalry, not doing chores, periodic attention-getting outbursts, or minor problems related to school.

We define serious behavior problems as those that severely challenge parental authority, are dangerous, self-destructive, or threaten the well-being of the family unit. Also, if your children engage in a number of minor problems, their behavior should be considered serious.

Please Note: None of the disciplinary consequences listed will be effective unless they are used in a consistent manner.

DISCIPLINARY CONSEQUENCES FOR MINOR BEHAVIOR PROBLEMS

Let's discuss the specific disciplinary consequences that you could find useful with minor behavior problems. Many of them, in all probability, are consequences that you have already used with your own children, but there are a few that may be new and prove useful to you. Again, use only those consequences you feel are appropriate for your family!

Separation: When the child is disruptive or will not cooperate, the child is separated from you and others into a nonstimulating, boring situation: standing in a corner, sitting in his or her room. The child should initially be given approximately the number of minutes of separation equal to his or her age; for example, a six-year-old should be given six minutes. If possible, use a kitchen timer to monitor the amount of time to be served. Tell your child, "You will stay in your room (or in the corner) until the bell goes off." The timer will help handle the yells of "When can I come out?" and prevent a parent, under some circumstances, from forgetting the child. If your child creates a disturbance while being separated, add more time. "Whenever you jump around while you are in the corner, you will stay another minute." Separation is a useful disciplinary consequence for children from ages approximately two to eleven.

Examples: Separate a three-year-old in the corner for three minutes for refusing to leave you alone while you were on the phone.

Separate a five-year-old in his or her room for five minutes for arguing with you.

Separate a seven-year-old for seven minutes for grabbing his brother's toys.

Word of warning: Some children will not stay in their rooms when placed there. Make sure you keep the child in his or her room and that you add more time if he or she leaves. You may want to remove games, toys, radio, TV, stereo, etc., from the room, so that the child will not have entertainment.

Comment: Separation is probably one of the best disciplinary consequences to use with pre-school and school-age children. Children "hate" not being part of the action. It is a gentle, yet highly effective consequence.

Taking Away Privileges: Taking away privileges includes suspending the right to watch TV, eat snacks, play with toys, participate in sports, use the telephone or stay up late. Parents usually suspend privileges by degrees: no TV for one night, then two nights, then all week. Whenever possible, the privilege taken away should relate to the nature of the problem. You forbid TV-watching because your child watched TV instead of doing homework. You take away use of the telephone because your teenager spoke longer than was allowed.

Examples: You take away for one week your eleven-year-old son's right to have friends over because he and his friend made a mess in the back yard.

You take away your seven-year-old's bike for one week because he rode it into the street.

You take away snacks from your ten-year-old daughter because she ate doughnuts five minutes before dinner.

Word of warning: Be careful not to deny privileges for too short or too long a period of time. It's best to start with a short period of time— just one day—and build if the problem continues.

Comment: Taking away privileges can be an effective disciplinary consequence at all age levels from pre-school on.

Physical Actions: Actions speak louder than words! The most appropriate response to your child's misbehavior may simply be to go up to him or her and physically accomplish what you want.

Examples: You take the ashtray away from your toddler when he does not comply with your request to put it down.

You go to your eleven-year-old's room to turn down the stereo when she does not comply with your request to do so.

You take your four-year-old by the arm and make him clean up his toys when he refuses to do so.

You escort your six-year-old to the dinner table when she does not come when called.

You take the toy gun away from your eight-year-old when he will not stop firing it in the living room.

Word of warning: Do not use excessive force when moving your child. The goal is to back up your words with action, not to hurt or frighten the child. Be sure to give him or her a choice: "Go to your room or you choose to have me take you there." Finally, physical action is most appropriate with younger children, typically those up to the age of ten.

"Do What I Want First": Doing what you have asked first is a common-sense approach to management that all parents use. You tell the child that until he or she has complied with your request, the child cannot do something that he or she desires: "You cannot eat dinner until you wash your hands" or "You cannot go outside until your room is cleaned."

Examples: Your children cannot watch TV or go outside until their home-work is finished.

Your eight-year-old cannot have a snack until his chores are finished.

Children cannot eat breakfast until they are dressed and their beds are made.

Word of warning: Stick to your word. If you say that there will be no breakfast until the child is dressed, be prepared for the child to miss breakfast.

Comment: This is a mild consequence that works for all age levels.

Grounding: You restrict your child to his or her room, house, or yard. The length of the restriction and the severity are related to the severity of the problem behavior.

Examples: Yard grounding: The child is restricted to the house and backyard for one day because he went into the street without permission.

House grounding: The child is grounded in the house for two days for lying to you about where he went after school.

Word of warning: Don't overuse grounding—maximum, one week for house or yard. Also, grounding will not work for children who don't care to be out and around the neighborhood.

Comment: Grounding is a highly effective consequence for school-age children, including adolescents, if used consistently.

THE MOST COMMON MINOR PROBLEMS
AND HOW TO HANDLE THEM

Here are some typical minor problems parents encounter. We have provided you with examples of consequences that you may find useful with each problem.

Problem	Disciplinary Consequence
Your seven-year-old goes away from home without telling you.	You ground the child at home for the following two days.
Your nine-year-old disrupts and argues at the dinner table.	Your child finishes his dinner alone in his room.
Your children argue and fight over which TV program to watch.	Neither child is allowed to watch TV for the remainder of the evening.
Your six-year-old rides her bike into the street.	You take her bike away for three days.
Your four-year-old makes a mess in the family room with her toys and will not clean them up.	You clean up the toys and do not give them back to the child for three days.
Your eleven-year-old will not pick up the dirty clothes.	You clean up the dirty clothes and take the clothes away for one week.
Your thirteen-year-old and his friends mess up the living room.	They are not allowed to go into the living room.

Problem	Disciplinary Consequence
Your four-year-old acts up at the market.	She is sent to her room as soon as you return home.
Your six-year-old acts up at a restaurant.	He is sent to his room as soon as you return home.
Your ten-year-old continually sneaks sweets between meals.	The child is not allowed in the kitchen by himself.
Your three-year-old keeps whining and complaining.	The child is sent to the corner for several minutes.
Your four-year-old continually interrupts you when you are on the phone.	The child is made to stand in the corner away from you until you are off the phone.
Your three-year-old has a tantrum when she does not get her way.	She is carried to her room and left there until she calms down.
Your children argue and fight.	Each is sent to a separate room for an appropriate amount of time.
Your teenager constantly ties up the phone.	You take away the phone privileges for the following day.
Your teenager stays out after curfew.	She is grounded for one week.

Problem	Disciplinary Consequence
Your eight-year-old does not do his required chores after school.	The chores must be done as soon as the child comes home from school, and until they are finished, the child cannot play outside, watch TV, or have a snack.
Your eight-year-old will not take a shower.	His shower must be taken after dinner and until it is, he cannot play or watch TV.
Your eleven-year-old will not clean his room.	The child must have cleaned his room by Saturday morning or he is not allowed to leave his room that day.
Your twelve-year-old will not do his work at school.	His schoolwork must be finished at home before he is allowed to play or watch TV after school.
Your teenager will not do her homework.	Her homework must be finished before she is allowed to talk on the telephone.

DISCIPLINARY CONSEQUENCES FOR SERIOUS BEHAVIOR.

Now let's discuss some specific disciplinary consequences you could find useful with serious problems. You may find that some of the consequences previously mentioned for use with minor problems are also appropriate for use with serious problems. Again, use only those consequences you feel would be appropriate for your family!

"I Am Watching You": "Watching" is an extremely close monitoring of the children's actions. It may even include violating the children's privacy. This is necessary when the children have engaged in behavior of a serious nature outside of your supervision. The consequences are most effective when you tell the children *how* you will be watching: "I am going to come to your classroom to make sure you are behaving," but not when you will be doing so.

Examples: You tape-record your children after they have been severely disruptive with sitters and listen to the tape to determine who was acting up. You may also utilize the tape recorder at school if the children have been a problem in class.

You require your teenager to provide you with sales slips for all purchases after he was caught shoplifting.

You walk into your child's classroom unannounced (teacher and principal know) after becoming aware he has been refusing to cooperate with the teacher.

Word of warning: These consequences should be used only in severe situations. Children, especially teenagers, do not like their privacy being violated. Be sure to tell the children that you will "snoop" unless they choose to improve their behavior.

Comment: For some children, such methods are necessary to let them know you care about them and that you really do mean business.

Outside Help: There are times when you may want or need assistance from other adults in disciplining your children. They may include your spouse or ex-spouse, the teacher, the principal, the local law-enforcement authorities, or a trained counselor or therapist.

Examples: Your son is extremely disruptive and will not listen to you, so you tell him you will call his father at work and have his father come home to deal with him.

Your daughter will not listen to you, so you have your ex-husband talk with her.

You cannot get your daughter to do her homework, so you have her teacher make her finish it during free time at school.

You are unsuccessful in getting your child to behave, so you seek family counseling.

Word of warning: Outside help should be sought only when you have attempted all other means available to you. Whenever possible, it is best for the adult involved in the conflict with the children to handle it on his or her own.

Comment: In this day and age, with so many one-parent families, it is not uncommon for the parent to need outside assistance. Counseling, in particular, can be an invaluable aid in improving your relationship with your children.

Room Grounding: Room grounding is the most severe form of grounding. Your children are basically isolated in their rooms with no TV, stereo, telephone, games or toys. The children are allowed to leave the room only to attend school, go to the bathroom, and eat.

Examples: You room-ground your twelve-year-old for one day for cussing at you.

You room-ground your teenager for two days for sneaking out without permission.

You room-ground your eleven-year-old for two days for hitting and kicking his younger brother.

Word of warning: Don't overdo room grounding—a maximum of one or two days at a time is sufficient.

Comment: Room grounding is called for when children are a highly disruptive influence in the family. It should only be utilized after less severe consequences have been attempted.

Out-of-Home Grounding: When children are flagrantly disruptive and blatantly noncooperative, they are sent to be "grounded" for a few hours or days with a neighbor or a relative. These individuals must be cooperative and agree not to make the stay "fun." The children should be required to stay in the neighbor's or relative's house without TV, stereo, or toys. If the stay is to be for an extended period of time, the children should be allowed to leave only to go to school and come back.

Examples: Your ten-year-old is highly disruptive and will not stay grounded, so you make him spend the remainder of the day grounded at your neighbor's.

Your teenager will not listen to you or respond to your limits, so you have him grounded for two days with your ex-spouse.

Your teenager cusses and strikes you, so you have him grounded for two days with his aunt and uncle.

Word of warning: This is obviously a severe consequence and should always be a last resort. Use only with older children and adolescents.

Comment: Out-of-home grounding could have a dramatic impact with many children. Sending a child away can break a cycle of conflict that has developed over a long period of time between parent and child.

SERIOUS PROBLEM BEHAVIORS AND HOW TO HANDLE THEM

Here are some examples of serious problems that parents encounter and consequences that parents have found useful in dealing with them.

Problem	Disciplinary Consequence
Your teenage daughter continuously lies to you about where she is going.	You ground her in her room for two days.
Your eleven-year-old does failing work at school.	You forbid TV and sports until his grades improve.
Your ten-year-old disrupts the family dinner by angrily provoking his younger brother.	He finishes his meal in his bedroom.
Your twelve-year-old vandalizes a wall at school.	You make him clean it up and pay for damages out of his allowance.
Your eight-year-old is suspended from school.	He is made to stay in his room without TV or toys the entire time he is suspended.
Your twelve-year-old simply will not listen to you.	You arrange out-of-home grounding at the neighbor's for the remainder of the day.
Your seven-year-old willfully smashes his sister's toys.	He is made to pay for the toys out of his allowance.
Your teenage daughter's friends smoke marijuana at your house while you are away.	She is grounded and not allowed to have friends over again when you are not home, for three months.

Problem	Disciplinary Consequence
Your ten-year-old steals money from your wallet.	She is made to repay you with her allowance and is grounded.
Your ten-year-old maliciously and continuously provokes his brother and sister while watching TV.	He loses the right to be in the family room and watch TV for one week.

POSITIVE CONSEQUENCES

We will now discuss the positive consequences you can utilize in your Assertive Discipline Plan when your children do behave. Before we discuss positive consequences you will first need to decide which of your children's behaviors you will want to reinforce. We will list typical problem behaviors your children may engage in and the appropriate behavior that you desire and will want to reinforce.

Problem	Desired Behavior
Child leaves home without telling you.	Child asks permission to leave.
Child argues at the dinner table.	Child eats quietly.
Child argues and fights over which TV program to watch.	Child cooperates with other family members.
Child rides bike in the street.	Child rides bike where you want.
Child does not clean up toys.	Child cleans up toys.

Problem	Desired Behavior
Child leaves dirty clothes out.	Child cleans up clothes.
Child whines and complains in market.	Child is cooperative.
Child acts up at restaurant.	Child eats and behaves appropriately.
Child sneaks snacks between meals.	Child does not eat without permission.
Child constantly whines and complains.	Child talks in appropriate tone of voice.
Child continually interrupts you.	Child is quiet when you are talking.
Child has tantrums when he does not get his way.	Child cooperates and follows your directions.
Child does not get ready for bed.	Child gets ready for bed.
Child stays out after curfew.	Child comes home on time.
Child lies.	Child tells the truth.
Child goes to bed screaming and yelling.	Child goes to bed quietly.
Child argues and complains.	Child cooperates.
Child constantly demands attention.	Child plays by himself.

EFFECTIVE POSITIVE CONSEQUENCES FOR TYPICAL BEHAVIOR PROBLEMS

Here are examples of effective ways that you can back up your words with action when your children do behave.

Problem Behavior	Motivator for Behavior
Your nine-year-old disrupts and argues at the dinner table.	He is allowed to choose dessert if he behaves.
Your children argue and fight over which TV program to watch.	The children are given extra TV time if they cooperate.
Your six-year-old rides her bike into the street.	She is allowed to stay out later if she stays on the sidewalk.
Your four-year-old makes a mess in the family room with her toys and does not clean them up.	She is given a jellybean every time she cleans up.
Your eleven-year-old will not pick up his dirty clothes.	He earns an allowance for picking up his clothes.
Your four-year-old acts up in the market.	You allow him to choose a treat if he cooperates.
Your six-year-old acts up at the restaurant.	He is allowed to choose a dessert if he behaves cooperatively.
Your four-year-old continually interrupts you when you are on the phone.	You give her a happy-face sticker when she does not interrupt you.

Problem Behavior	Motivator for Behavior
Your three-year-old constantly whines and complains.	You provide her with a few peanuts every time she talks to you in an appropriate voice.
Your three-year-old has tantrums when he does not get his way.	You give him extra time with you when he cooperates.
Your four-year-old keeps getting out of bed.	You give him a happy-face sticker for staying in bed.
Your four-year-old will not share her toys.	You give her a few mints when she does share her toys.
Your five-year-old will not get ready for bed on time.	You read him a story when he does get ready for bed on time.
Your three-year-old becomes hysterical whenever you leave.	He gets a treat from the sitter if he does not cry.
Your four-year-old goes to bed every night crying and screaming.	She earns special time with you in the morning if she goes to bed quietly.
Your five-year-old will not play by herself. She constantly follows you around.	You let her earn extra time with you for story-reading when she plays by herself.
Your five-year-old continually comes into your room in the middle of the night.	He will earn a 10-cent toy plane each night that he sleeps in his room without coming out.

Problem Behavior	Motivator for Behavior
Your teenager continually lies to you about where she is going.	Every time you check with her and she has told you the truth, she earns a point. When she earns ten points, she may attend a party.
Your eleven-year-old does failing work at school.	Every day that his work is done at school, he earns a point. When he earns ten points, he may get his bike painted.
Your ten-year-old disrupts the family by angrily provoking his younger brother.	Every day that he does not provoke his brother, he earns a point. When he earns five points, he will be allowed to go to a movie.
Your eight-year-old is suspended from school.	Every day that he behaves at school, he earns a point. When he earns ten points, he may go fishing with his father.
Your twelve-year-old does not listen to you.	Every time that he cooperates, he earns a point. When he earns one hundred points, he will get a bonus on his allowance.
Your eleven-year-old continually lies to you.	Every day that he does not lie, he earns a point. When he earns fifteen points, he may go to the car races.

Problem Behavior	Motivator for Behavior
Your nine-year-old is very disruptive whenever the family is together.	He earns a point for every hour that he is quiet and co-operative. When he earns thirty points, he may go to the toy store and buy a small toy.
Your six-year-old cries and screams and does not want to go to school.	You put a surprise treat in his lunch box each day that he goes to school without getting upset.
Your five-year-old con-stantly complains about physical ailments that are not real.	You allow her special time for playing with her favorite toy each day that she does not complain.

Appendix 2 **WORKSHEETS**

Discipline Plan Worksheet (Step Three)

Which specific behaviors do you and your spouse feel your child MUST change?

        Child's Name _____

        1st behavior: _____

        2nd behavior: _____

Which Disciplinary Consequence will you use?
        For example: send to room, take away privileges, no TV, toys, friends over, phone, allowance, etc.)
        See Appendix 1, pages 102-113, for suggestions.
        Consequence _____
If this consequence does not work, which stronger consequence will you use? _____
_____

If you are using a Discipline Hierarchy, what consequence(s) will you provide your child?

        The 1st time he/she misbehaves _____

        _____

        The 2nd time he/she misbehaves _____

        _____

        The 3rd time he/she misbehaves _____

        _____

(continued)

The 4th time he/she misbehaves _____

_____

If your child misbehaves when you are not present, how will you monitor the problem behavior?

☐ Telephone

☐ Neighbor visit
Who? _____

☐ Tape record

☐ Written note from teacher

How will you support your children's appropriate behavior? _____

_____

Positive Reinforcement Worksheet

If you are not sure what rewards would most motivate your children, sit down with them, one at a time, and ask them the following questions:

What do you like to do best with Mother? _____

_____

What do you like to do best with Father? _____

_____

Who would you like to spend more time with? _____

_____

(continued)

Suggestions:

Mother	Uncle
Father	Friend
Grandmother	Other

What would you like to do more often at home? _____

_____

Suggestions:

Have friends over	Use parents' tools, tape
Pick TV programs	player, etc.
Stay up later	Rent video movies
Select food for dinner	Play special games
Play sports	Do arts and crafts projects
Have party	Do hobbies
	Other

Suggestions you could use _____

Other _____

_____

_____

Parent Saver Worksheet

If you plan to use a Positive Contract, use this worksheet.

What behavior(s) do you want your child to engage in?

_____

_____

What will you provide your child when he/she behaves?
(E.g., point, star.) _____

_____

(continued)

How many points, stars, etc., will it take to earn the reward? _____

_____

What reward will the child earn? _____

_____

If you plan to use Marble Mania, what reward(s) will the children earn? _____

_____

_____

How many marbles will they have to earn to get the reward? _____

_____

Help from Spouse Worksheet

Before asking your spouse for help use this worksheet.

Goal for conversation (I need your help with the children, etc.) _____

_____

_____

What do you specifically want your spouse to do? _____

_____

_____

_____

(continued)

Rationale for why you are talking to spouse. _____

_____

_____

_____

Consequences you feel will occur if he/she does not help you. _____

_____

_____

_____

Teacher-Parent Assertive Discipline Plan Worksheet

If your child is having problems behaving in class, have his/her teacher(s) fill out this form.

What rules do you want my child to obey in your classroom?

1. _____

2. _____

3. _____

4. _____

5. _____

What will you do the first time my child breaks one of your rules? _____

What will you do the second time my child breaks one of your rules? _____

What will you do the third time my child breaks one of your rules? _____

(continued)

What will you do the fourth time my child breaks one of your rules? _____

What will you do the fifth time my child breaks one of your rules? _____

What will you do when my child follows your rules?

_____

How do you want me to support your efforts? _____

_____

Administrator-Parent Assertive Discipline Plan Worksheet

If your child is having problems behaving outside of class in the school, the halls, yard, etc., have the principal, vice-principal or counselor fill out this form.

What rules do you want my child to obey in the halls, in the yard, etc.?

1. _____
2. _____
3. _____
4. _____
5. _____

What will you do the first time my child breaks one of your rules? _____

What will you do the second time my child breaks one of your rules? _____

(continued)

What will you do the third time my child breaks one of your rules? _____

What will you do the fourth time my child breaks one of your rules? _____

What will you do the fifth time my child breaks one of your rules? _____

What will you do when my child follows your rules?

_____

How do you want me to support your efforts? _____

_____

Home-School Assertive Discipline Plan Worksheet

If your child is having problems in school, use this worksheet. It will help you determine how to monitor and follow up on your child's behavior in school.

How will you monitor your child's behavior at school?
Note _____Phone Call _____Other_____

What disciplinary consequences will you provide your child if he/she misbehaves at school? _____

_____

What positive consequence will you provide your child if he/she behaves at school? _____

_____

Appendix 3 ASSERTIVE DISCIPLINE FOR PARENTS WORKSHOPS

Assertive Discipline for Parents Workshops are available in most communities in the United States and Canada. These Workshops are a must for all parents who want additional help in dealing effectively with the behavior of children.

Assertive Discipline for Parents Workshops are sponsored by schools, PTA's, PTO's, church or temple groups, adult education programs, etc.

If you are interested in attending or in receiving training for conducting Assertive Discipline for Parents Workshops, please contact:

Canter & Associates, Inc.
PO Box 2113
Santa Monica, CA 90406

(213) 395-3221